STARTING CRUISING
A Complete Manual

RODNEY WILLETT

DAVID & CHARLES
Newton Abbot   London

HIPPOCRENE BOOKS INC
New York

For R. J. and K. W.

British Library Cataloguing in Publication Data

Willett, Rodney
  Starting cruising.
  1. Boats and boating
  I. Title
  797.1   GV775

  ISBN 0-7153-8401-5 (Great Britain)
  ISBN 0-88254-832-8 (United States)

Typeset by Typesetters (Birmingham) Limited
Edgbaston Road, Smethwick, Warley, West Midlands
and printed in Great Britain
by Butler & Tanner Limited, Frome and London
for David & Charles (Publishers) Limited
Brunel House Newton Abbot Devon

Contents

	Introduction	7
1	Anchors and Anchoring	9
2	Anchor Handling and Stowing	26
3	Mooring, Berthing, Warping and Slow-speed Working	36
4	Pilotage and Basic Navigation	52
5	The Navigator's Tools and Equipment	77
6	The Signposts of the Sea	100
7	The Tides	109
8	Weather Forecasting and Bad-weather Tactics	116
9	The Rules of the Road and Communications	126
10	Radio and Electronic Aids	143
11	Services	147
12	The Crew	165
	Appendices	
I	Clothing	180
II	First-aid and Seasickness	181
III	Emergency-gear Checklist	184
IV	Rescue Services	186
	Bibliography and Useful Addresses	188
	Index	191

The author and publishers would like to thank Peter Cook, editor of *Yachts and Yachting*, for his permission to use material which has appeared, either in part or in whole, in that magazine. They would also like to thank B. T. Batsford Ltd for permission to use the extract from Colin Mudie's article 'Left Foot, Right Foot' which is taken from the anthology *The Yachtsman's Bedside Book* edited by Frank Snoxell (Batsford, 1965).

Introduction

This book is about cruising – and especially about cruising with a family including small children. Its aim is to help those who have experience of dinghy or day-boat sailing to extend their knowledge. It is assumed, therefore, that the reader already possesses a good working knowledge of sailing and general boatmanship.

There is a real difference between the approach of the small-boat sailor, whether he races or not, and the cruising man who spends long periods aboard. For one thing the day sailor has no real objection to becoming wet and cold, secure in the knowledge that he will be able to take a bath or shower on his return ashore. The cruising man, on the other hand, will do all in his power to keep his crew (himself included) from becoming wetter or colder than is strictly necessary. Apart from the problems associated with drying wet clothing on board there is the question of safety – a cold or wet crew is an inefficient crew and an inefficient crew is generally an unsafe crew.

There is also a difference in attitude between the racing man and the cruising man. The racing man will push both boat and crew as hard as possible. This is fine when the racing is accompanied by safety boats, as is usual when dinghies race, or takes place where there is company. This is not the place to argue the rights and wrongs of ocean racing but it is not a part of the cruising man's sport to risk the lives of his crew or of those who may become involved in trying to save them. He must operate as if he is entirely alone and be prepared for any eventuality.

Colin Mudie once wrote:

To my dismay I found that a comfortable passage was as important to the cruising man, even more so perhaps, than driving the boat to its knees against the fury of the elements. To this day I fidget at the very conception. Worse was yet to come for at breakfast the draught from the great outdoors was enough to blow the rice krispies off the plates to snap and popple in the bilge unseen. My host, the owner, actually went upstairs and *stopped the boat*. We hove-to for breakfast, the motion went mild as if by magic, the krispies band played noisily on each plate and life was different. No other single act of seamanship has ever made such an impression on me. Until that moment I had no idea how ingrained in me was the idea that once you left moorings you sailed, full belt and willy nilly, until you came to those other moorings placed not far from The Finish. Most gloomy tales of loss or disaster to sailing yachts in open water have this background theme of the tired crew driving on and on to their doom rather than stopping for a cup of tea and a snooze.

I can think of no better way of illustrating the cruising man's philosophy. Cruising should be a pleasure – a pleasure for all on board from hardened skipper to nervous nine-year-old. This pleasure is a strange mixture, appealing as it does to the explorer, to those seeking peace and respite from the pace of modern life, to those who wish to be close to nature and to the seaman who derives great satisfaction from making a safe and uneventful passage.

Much has been written about safety. Unfortunately there has arisen a real confusion between safety equipment and emergency equipment. Safety equipment enables you to go from A to B without an accident; emergency equipment is there for use when things have gone wrong. In this book you will not find any section solely devoted to safety as it is brought in at every stage. Emergency equipment is covered in Chapter 8 which deals with heavy weather.

Most books introducing the reader to cruising devote a chapter to choosing a suitable boat. Although interesting, these are rarely helpful; apart from anything else, few of us can afford the sort of boat usually chosen as an example. The only advice that can be given is to look at and go on board as many boats as possible before you buy. All cruising boats are a compromise. The more you see, and the more owners you talk to, the better will be your chance of selecting the right compromise for your needs and your proposed cruising area.

I hope that you will find this book makes both pleasant armchair reading and a useful reference book afloat. If, as a result of reading it, you enjoy the true freedom of cruising that I have enjoyed, then I will have achieved my objective.

Yacht *Wanderer*   Rodney Willett
Frogmore Creek
South Devon

1
Anchors and Anchoring

One of the basic differences between the day-sailer and the cruising boat is that the latter will spend a great deal of time at anchor as opposed to being on her permanent mooring or marina berth. Before we look at the types of anchor available to us and at the different techniques and methods we can employ, it is worth looking at the various jobs for which we carry this tackle. At every stage we must remember that we are looking for both safety and enjoyment – with the emphasis on the former.

We have made a fast passage from the port where we spent last night to an estuary we have never visited before, and which we wish to explore. It is nearly lunchtime as we work up the estuary and we know that we shall have to wait for the tide before we can reach its head and so we decide to stop for lunch. We drop our lightest anchor, the kedge, which the Americans often refer to as the 'lunch hook'. This anchor is shackled to a short length of chain, about two metres, and a light nylon rode or cable so that it is easy to handle. It will probably hold us and is perfectly safe as we are on board ready for action should it drag.

Later that evening, having explored the estuary and the town at its head, we are back at the mouth of the river ready for an early start next morning. There are no handy visitors' moorings so we must anchor for the night. For this job we choose our main working anchor, the bower. Heavier than the kedge, this anchor is shackled to a longer length of chain, about 10m, backed with a nylon cable for use in deep water. It will be harder to weigh than the kedge but is well worth the effort as the crew can turn in with a sense of security – even if the skipper does sleep with half an ear open just in case.

Next day we set off according to plan but then everything seems to go wrong. The forecast is for gales later but now the wind drops away just when we need it to make our next port before the weather deteriorates. Soon we realise that, even with help from our small auxiliary engine, we shall be a long way from our destination when the wind rises. A quick look at the chart shows that there is a cove nearby which will offer shelter. We decide to make for it rather than ride out the storm; after all we aren't on holiday just to prove our-selves by getting soaked to the skin and tired out. This time we choose our heaviest anchor with its all-chain rode or cable – our storm anchor. Once satisfied that this is holding, we prepare the working anchor just in case we need it for extra holding power. Then we go below for a hot drink.

Thus we are carrying three anchors to meet the three types of situation that we are likely to encounter. Furthermore, should we have to slip – or should we lose – one anchor, there is another available. In short, we are prepared for anything.

There are various types of anchor available on the market, each having its own different characteristics: different holding characteristics, depending on the nature of the sea bed (the holding ground); different weighing and handling problems and different stowage requirements.

The rodes or cables which attach the anchor to the boat serve two purposes. Obviously they must be strong enough to hold anchor and boat together. Their second job is just as important: it is to transmit the pull from the boat to the anchor in such a way that the latter's holding power is not reduced. We will look at this later.

At all times we must remember that cruising is meant to be fun and not hard work. The gear should be as light and easy to handle as possible under normal conditions – but heavy enough to ensure that we stay put even in severe conditions. As always we must compromise but, as ground tackle is one of the most important safety items we carry, we must compromise with great care; know as much about the subject as we can before choosing the equipment and then practise the various anchoring techniques until we are as efficient as possible. Standing on a pitching foredeck in the dark trying to sort things out as a lee shore looms ever closer is not the time to find something has gone wrong!

Anchors

Types of Anchor

We are all familiar with the fisherman anchor (see Fig 1.1). It works because, regardless of how it falls on the sea bed, as soon as it is pulled by the cable the wide stock turns it over so that one of the flukes digs into the ground. These flukes are small in area and the resistance offered in soft holding grounds is correspondingly small. Furthermore, one fluke is left standing up in the water and the cable can become wrapped round it if the boat swings right round the anchor (see Fig 1.2). When this happens the anchor has no holding power at all. To overcome these problems a number of so-called patent anchors have been designed. However, the fisherman remains the best anchor when over rock and will penetrate kelp or thick coverings of weed which tend to become wrapped around the point

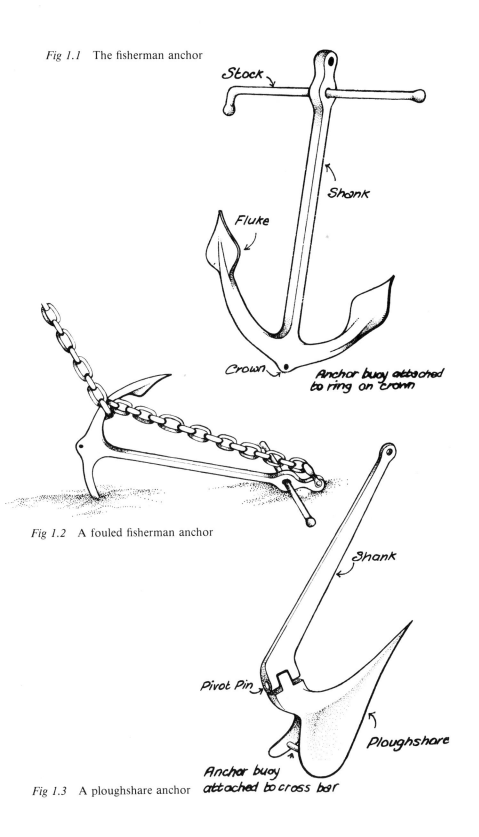

Fig 1.1   The fisherman anchor

Stock

Shank

Fluke

Crown

Anchor buoy attached
to ring on crown

Fig 1.2   A fouled fisherman anchor

Shank

Pivot Pin

Ploughshare

Anchor buoy
attached to cross bar

Fig 1.3   A ploughshare anchor

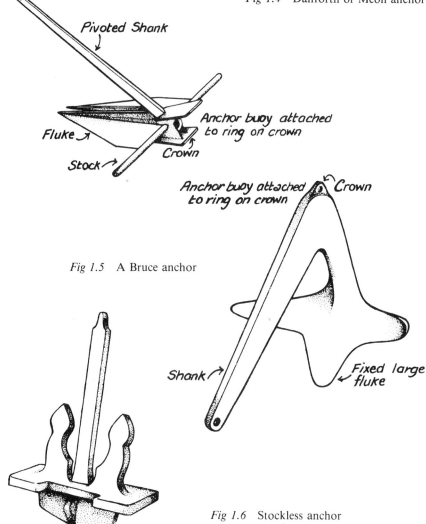

Fig 1.4   Danforth or Meon anchor

Pivoted Shank

Fluke

Stock

Crown

Anchor buoy attached to ring on crown

Fig 1.5   A Bruce anchor

Anchor buoy attached to ring on crown

Crown

Shank

Fixed large fluke

Fig 1.6   Stockless anchor

of patent anchors before they penetrate the bottom. For this reason, many people still carry this type of anchor.

The first patent anchor to become popular, and rightly so, was the plough type (see Fig 1.3). This anchor consists of two ploughshares mounted back-to-back and fitted to a long shank so that the ploughs can pivot within set limits. The strains on this type of anchor are considerable and its ability to dig into the holding ground depends on the angle the plough tip makes with the sea bed when it is lying in its natural attitude. The original (known as the CQR – secure) is manufactured by Simpson-Lawrence of Glasgow and fulfils both those requirements. A number of other firms manufacture plough anchors but some, although not all, are of inferior design or manufacture and should be avoided at all costs. If you opt for an alternative to the CQR make certain that it is Lloyds Approved.

Meanwhile, in the United States, another patent anchor was developed known as the Danforth (see Fig 1.4). These anchors consist of two large flukes mounted close together on a stock, all pivoted on a long shank. The angle of the flukes as it lies on the bottom is important if this anchor is to dig in quickly. Once dug in, the large flukes give the anchor tremendous holding power limited more by its strength than by its weight. It follows that they must be strongly made and one often sees inferior Danforth types with bent and buckled flukes or stocks. Isaiah Preston of Warley now hold the sole manufacturing rights of the Danforth in this country – they call it the 'Meon' – but a number of other companies manufacture similar anchors to Lloyds Approval requirements.

A number of other patent anchors were developed but none was really satisfactory (some were even dangerous) until the Bruce came along (see Fig 1.5). This was designed in the first place for holding static loads, such as oil rigs, with the shortest possible scope (or length) of cable. There is no question about its suitability for this task but opinions vary as to its use on cruising boats. The absence of moving parts and the ability to hold on short scopes are plus factors. I have a small one for the dinghy and am very pleased with it for that duty. Never having used one on a larger boat I must rely on other people's experiences; some tell of being unable to dig the anchor into the bed and of the anchor dragging rather unexpectedly, but others state they are very happy with the Bruce despite the fact that it is not the easiest anchor to stow. Certainly, if I used a Bruce for either the bower or storm anchor, I would carry a plough or Danforth for the other. The Bruce will hold on most rocky holding grounds and so could well replace the fisherman usually used as a kedge.

There are, of course, other types of anchor such as mushroom, grapnel and rond. None of these is suited to the duties under consideration, being designed for either permanent moorings or inland waterways. However, there is one other type a few cruising men consider. This is the stockless anchor as used on large commercial craft where weight is no problem. These must be far heavier than any of the other anchors for the same holding power but will self-stow in a hawse pipe without attention. This means that the boat must be fitted with hawse pipes – an unusual feature – and may need a heavier winch than would normally be fitted. Both Isaiah Preston and Simpson-Lawrence manufacture a range of stockless anchors suited for small craft (see Fig 1.6).

Holding Power
The holding power of the various types of anchor varies according to the type of holding ground. Table 1.1 offers a guide and will help you to decide which type(s) to choose for your cruising ground.

Table 1.1   Holding Power of Various Anchors on Various Holding Grounds

Anchor	*Mud*	*Sand*	*Gravel*	*Hard bottom*	*Rock*
Fisherman	Poor	Poor	Poor	Good	Good
Plough	Good	Excellent	Good	Poor	Poor
Danforth	Excellent	Excellent	Good	Poor	Poor
Bruce	Good	Good	Good	Fair	Fair

Stockless anchors, by virtue of their weight, are suitable over a wide variety of holding grounds but the manufacturer's advice should be sought before making a purchase.

The Cable or Rode
We have already noted that the cable must present the pull from the boat in such a way as to maintain maximum holding power. With the possible exception of the Bruce anchor, this means that the pull on the anchor must be nearly horizontal and should be as steady as possible so the cable must act as a spring to take out the shock loads as the boat's weight is thrown onto it.

An all-chain cable fulfils these requirements as it falls in a deep curve, or catenary, which takes most of the shock loading out of the system as it lifts up. Its weight is important, adding to the overall holding power. However, although easy to stow, chains are heavy to handle and an all-chain cable is needed only on the storm anchor so long as the minimum amounts are fitted to the other anchors, ie 2m on the kedge and 10m on the main working anchor. The rope warp used to back up the chain should be of nylon as this will stretch as the load is applied and so reduce the shock loading. The size must be chosen with care – too small and it will break, too large and it will fail to act as a spring.

Incidentally, this question of ironing out the shock loads is also important for the crew's comfort. Life on board a boat that is constantly snubbing at her anchor soon loses its charm and can make handling hot food and drink both difficult and dangerous.

The amount of cable to let go – the scope – depends on the maximum depth of the water at high tide and the conditions. If all chain is used it will be a minimum of three times the maximum depth, rising to five times in severe conditions. These figures become five and eight when using rope. Thus our main working anchor with 10m of chain can be used in depths of up to just over 3m without backing it up with nylon rope. Thereafter, 5m of nylon should be let go for each additional metre in depth.

Cable, be it chain or rope, should be stowed with great care. The time may well come when it is required in a hurry and, although a wise skipper will always overhaul (ie pull out and flake down ready) the cable before the anchor is let go if there is time, in an emergency it is annoying to find the anchor hanging just over the bows held there by a tangle of chain in the chain locker. Although chain will self-stow in the locker, it will do so into a pyramid which will almost certainly capsize at sea and refuse to run out smoothly. If possible a crew member should be detailed below when the anchor is being weighed to flake the chain down carefully so that it is stable.

Rope cables can be stowed on reels, but if this is not possible they must be carefully coiled and hung up or stowed in bags. Coastguards stow their cliff ropes in kitbags by flaking them down into the bag and then tying the bag loosely around the rope. Put a stop knot in both ends of the rope to prevent the end going in and the bitter end from being lost. If done properly the rope will feed out easily.

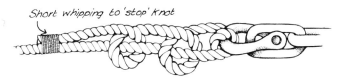

Fig 1.7   Round turn and two half hitches with whipping to 'stop' knot

The bitter end of the chains on storm anchors should be tied using either a round turn and two half hitches or a bowline – in both cases the knots should be 'stopped' as shown in Fig 1.7 – with a length of nylon line, the same size as used on the main anchor is ideal, to a fixing in the bottom of the chain locker. This line must be long enough to feed out onto the deck so that, if anything happens, it can be cut through to slip the anchor. The chain must never be shackled into the locker – when the strain comes onto it it will be impossible to undo it and, in any event, there may not be time to go below to deal with it. The best way to deal with the main working anchor is to fit the chain with a similar line but to use a shackle to attach it to the chain so that it can be undone when using the backing nylon cable. This too can be cut if necessary.

Suitable sizes of cables are shown in Table 1.2. Although suggested minimum lengths are shown, the length required depends on the depth of the water and not the size of the boat. However, these lengths will cover most cruising requirements around the United Kingdom. Naturally, winch gypsies (and fairleads) must be of a suitable size and may influence the size chosen. If these fittings really are too small, they may have to be changed.

Table 1.2   **Suggested Sizes of Cables**

Boat LOA (ft)	Storm Anchor		Main Anchor			Kedge Anchor		
	Chain dia (in)	Length (m)	Chain dia (in)	Rope dia (mm)	Length (m)	Chain dia (in)	Rope dia (mm)	Length (m)
15	¼	35	¼	10	35	¼	10	10
20	¼	40	¼	12	40	¼	10	15
25	⁵⁄₁₆	45	⁵⁄₁₆	14	45	¼	12	18
30	½	50	½	16	50	⁵⁄₁₆	14	20
40	⁷⁄₁₆	50	⁷⁄₁₆	18	50	⁵⁄₁₆	14	20

Notes These figures are all minimum sizes based on a medium-displacement boat of the length shown anchored in reasonable sheltered conditions. There is much to be said for erring on the heavy side when looking at chain but the rope warps will not offer the right amount of 'spring' if increased much above the sizes shown. Throughout, it is assumed that the main anchors are fitted with 10 metres of chain, the balance being rope, and kedges with 2 metres of chain; it is also assumed that the chain is of the short-link type and that rope cables are 8-strand plaited nylon.

Before You Anchor

By now it will be obvious that we must know the depth of water below us and the nature of the holding ground before we can anchor. It is wise to make a trial run, or runs, over the proposed anchorage to check both even though the chart may well provide you with the information you need – assuming you know exactly where you are!

Most people will use the echo sounder as this will give the depth and a fair idea of the nature of the sea bed if you know what to look for. The display will differ as follows:

Soft Mud   The gain control will be set high to eliminate unwanted echoes. The leading edge of the display will be rather indefinite and woolly.

Rocks   The echo is long and broken up regardless of changes made to the gain control. The leading edge will change rapidly as the boat moves over the rocks.

Sand, Gravel   The gain control will be set low as these bottoms give the strongest and clearest echoes. There will probably be a number of rebound echoes.

Although the echo sounder will give you the facts you require, they have been known to play false. The simplest and best device for this job is still the lead-line. Armed with tallow to give you a sample from the sea bed, you receive accurate information with nothing to go wrong. All cruising boats should carry a lead – you never know when the echo sounder is going to fail – and tallow, still one of the best sea-going lubricants on the market. However, using a lead does demand a certain amount of skill which can be acquired only by practice.

Having determined the nature of the holding ground, we select the right anchor for the job in hand. In practice this will depend on the conditions and the length of time we intend to stay rather than the state of the holding ground unless it is unsuitable for the anchor we have chosen. We also need to decide whether or not we are going to use an anchor buoy.

The anchor buoy is attached to the crown of the anchor by a line called a tripping line. Most anchors, and all good ones, are fitted with an eye for this purpose. The function of the tripping line is to enable us to retrieve the anchor without difficulty even if it has become fouled under an old mooring chain or other obstruction by pulling it out the same way as it went in. It also enables us to retrieve the anchor if we have had to slip it for any reason. Incidentally, it can help to bring the anchor aboard without damaging the topsides in certain boats.

It is said that tripping lines and anchor buoys are not easy to set as they tend to tangle around the main cable; that the lines are often cut by the propellers of passing boats and that other folk pick them up thinking they are mooring buoys. These problems can be overcome. If there is a short length, say 2m, of light chain shackled to the buoy before the tripping line is attached, the buoy may be thrown over before the anchor is let go and will usually drift clear so avoiding a tangle with the cable. This chain will also solve the problem of the passing propeller. To avoid misuse the buoy should carry the name of the boat and the words ANCHOR BUOY – DO NOT MOOR. This will deter most folk even if they don't know what an anchor buoy is!

No one can deny that setting an anchor buoy takes more trouble than not using one, which is why few are seen today. However, few of our anchorages are free from old chain and other rubbish on the bottom and the trouble required to set a buoy is as nothing to that caused by a fouled anchor. At sea, where the bottom should be clear of debris, there is always the slight possibility that you will have to slip or that the anchor may be lost in a moment of panic. It is nice to know, in these circumstances, that the anchor is already buoyed and can be retrieved later rather than to mourn the two hundred pounds or so worth of anchor and cable that has departed from your life.

Knowing the depth below and having calculated the maximum depth at high tide, we know how much cable to veer. We can, of course, drag it out on deck until we have the required amount – indeed, we may have to do that if it has been badly stowed. However, life is easier if the cable has been marked in some fashion so that we know how much we have let go. Some winches are fitted with counters to give us the answer, as we shall see in Chapter 2. However, we may prefer to mark the cable itself and, since all modern charts give depths in metres, we may as well use the metric system. Choose two colours of paint that contrast well – such as white and red – and paint links in accordance with Table 1.3. Note that the links painted indicate the amount of cable below the water line when the painted links are on the winch gypsy or against some other mark on deck. This means checking the distance from water line to gypsy before you start. Since it is very boring to have to wait for paint to dry, use one of the aerosol car paints or something similar. It doesn't matter if the links aren't properly painted so long as they are marked.

Table 1.3   Marking Cables and Lead Lines

Depth in metres	Marking
2	1 white
4	2 white
6	3 white
8	4 white
10	1 red
12	1 red + 1 white
14	1 red + 2 white
16	1 red + 3 white
18	1 red + 4 white
20	2 red
25	2 red + 1 white
30	3 red
35	3 red + 1 white
40	4 red etc

Rope cables can be marked using the same system but with whippings made from different coloured twine. Incidentally, you can mark the lead line the same way. The traditional code, attractive though it is, demands a feat of memory which is beyond most people unless they are using it almost every day.

Anchoring Techniques

Anchoring to a single anchor is the most usual and simplest method. Ideally, having chosen the place where the anchor is to be dropped, the boat passes over that place, stops and makes sternway. As she starts to go astern, the anchor buoy is thrown over, followed by the anchor. The appropriate amount of cable is pulled out as the boat moves astern; this is made fast and the boat brought up by it thus ensuring that it has dug into the holding ground and that the cable is lying in a straight line from boat to anchor with no tangles. For this reason anchors must not be let go when the boat is stationary as the cable ends up in a glorious muddle on top of itself. Using engine power, this manoeuvre is simple – especially if the boat is turned into the flow before stopping, which is always advisable to avoid the boat swinging on her anchor as soon as power is taken off (unless the boat is more likely to be wind rode in which case turn into the wind rather than the flow). Under sail life can be rather more complicated.

If wind and tide are in the same direction, life is simple. Approach close hauled, turn up into the wind and let the elements stop the boat and take her back. As soon as the anchor is holding and the boat has settled, stow the sails. This is fine, but we are rarely fortunate enough to meet such perfect conditions. How you act when wind and tide are not together depends to a great extent on the boat and how she behaves – which can be found only by trial and error. If she has a shallow draught and is likely to be wind rode, the above technique can be used ignoring the flow. However, even shallow-draught boats will be affected to some extent by the current and it depends on the relative strength of wind and water just what will happen. If wind is against tide and tide will have the greater effect, approach up wind with headsails only. Let the sheets fly (or furl the sail if you have roller furling) and let the tide do the rest of the work. If tide and wind are at an angle to each other it may prove easier to make a flying anchorage by sailing down the tide. This should be done as slowly as possible and it is usually safer to use headsails alone. As you sail over the place where the anchor is to be dropped, throw over the buoy and let go the anchor. When the appropriate amount of cable has been pulled out – note the word 'pulled' – make fast the cable. If you are going too fast this will be hard work. Let fly the sheets and let the boat's momentum pull the anchor into the ground. The boat will then swing round to face the anchor. If you have approached with main as well as headsails, sheet in the main to try to ensure that she swings away from the wind. Otherwise . . . well you can see why it's safer using headsails alone.

Some books give pretty diagrams showing you how to anchor under sail in various conditions. Although the theory is sound, I have yet to sail in the boat that behaves according to the book. There is no substitute for trying things out in a nice secluded space until you are sure you know how your boat will react under almost any set of circumstances. If you spend about six hours – ideally from full flood to full ebb – on a day when the wind is steady, just stopping the boat and seeing how she falls away, you will learn more than sixty hours reading, no matter how experienced the author.

Assuming that there is ample room to swing and that conditions are not so severe as to drag the anchor, there is little point in using more than one; after all, it is hard enough to weigh one anchor when you want to leave.

However carefully we choose our anchorage (the rule is to anchor near other similar craft using similar cables, ie deep-keel boats using all-chain cables, shallow-draught boats with high topsides such as motor cruisers using rope cables etc) the time will come when we cannot find a large enough space to swing safely. We must, therefore, use a second anchor to reduce our need for space. There are two methods.

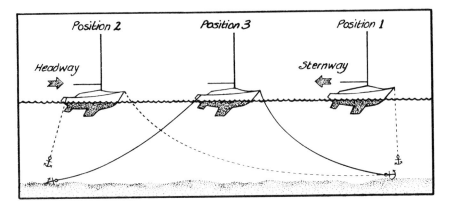

Fig 1.8   Moored fore and aft between two anchors. The boat should be anchored with her bow towards strongest current

The first method is to anchor fore and aft (see Fig 1.8). Drop and set the first anchor as described above and then veer twice as much cable as would usually be required. Drop a second anchor – the kedge is usually big enough – over the stern and either haul the boat forward on the main anchor cable while letting go aft or use the engine to take her forward. When the boat is centred, make fast both cables. The heaviest anchor should be laid towards the strongest flow – usually the ebb if backed by a river – so if the weakest flow is running when you anchor you must do everything the other way

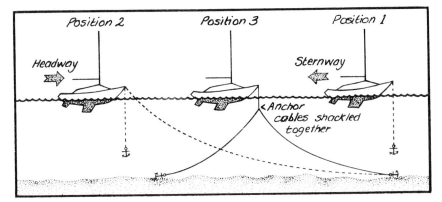

Fig 1.9   Swinging between two anchors. Anchors should be laid in line with the main current, with the heaviest laid towards strongest flow

around; laying the kedge first and dropping back on that, then taking the kedge cable aft so that the boat swings right round before dropping down on the current so the main anchor can be laid.

The second method is to moor between two anchors (see Fig 1.9). Frankly, I would only advise this when conditions are bad enough to make the first method unsafe or if the boat is to remain at anchor for some time. The usual method is to lay the main anchor as above and drop back twice the usual distance, drop the second anchor over the bow and haul or motor back to the centre point. Next shackle the second cable to the first and drop the join over the bow so that it is hanging below the keel to avoid the keel fouling the cables as the boat swings. This description ignores the fact that the chances of the cable on the second anchor being the right length are remote. If you attach the two cables together and bring both on board you can end up with an interesting tangle under your bow if the boat swings around her mooring a few times – especially if you are unlucky enough to include a floating branch in the tangle as once happened to me.

I prefer to use the storm anchor as the first one over the bow and then to drop back the distance required plus 10m (the amount of chain on the main anchor). Drop the main anchor and haul back until you reach the end of the main anchor chain and then shackle that onto the storm anchor chain. Drop the join below the keel and the job is done. Even this isn't ideal as there should be a swivel between the join and the boat but there is no way that this can be achieved.

When we are exposed to severe weather, the storm anchor may not be able to hold us on its own and will need assistance. You will read that the first option when the anchor drags is to lay out more cable. Then it is suggested that a weight be dropped down the cable to improve the spring effect so as to ensure that the pull on the anchor remains horizontal and has most of the shock loading taken out of it. Both methods are perfectly sound, the main problem being that it takes time to organise a weight and to find a shackle large enough to run down the cable – even if there is one on board to find. The second problem is that, if these measures fail to stop you dragging, there is first a weight and then a long cable to haul aboard before you can take further action – hard work on a pitching foredeck, even if you use the engine to help. It is often easier, and safer, to lay a second anchor. Again we have two options. The first is to haul in – use the engine to take the boat ahead as you haul – until the scope is rather more than the maximum depth plus 12m. Shackle the end of the main anchor chain to the storm anchor chain and let go the main anchor. When the main anchor has either found the sea bed or is hanging up and down, veer more cable until you have a total scope of four times the depth minimum (see Fig 1.10). The reason for hauling in until you

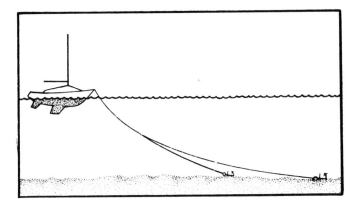

Fig 1.10 Lying to two anchors: method 1. Note that the second anchor is shackled to main chain so that the length of chain from the first anchor to the shackle is about twice the maximum depth

have the amount shown above before attaching the second anchor is that you want to avoid having to weigh both anchors at once as would happen if the scope was reduced further. This method will give you about twice the holding power of one anchor. A neater way, which can be used if the maximum depth will not exceed about 8m and you decide to start off using two anchors, is to let the main anchor go first and attach the end of its chain to the storm anchor cable about 2m from the storm anchor. This, however, can be used only in a limited number of circumstances.

When using the second method we don't touch the storm anchor cable at all. We use the engine (or sails, but engine is a lot easier) to take the boat forward and to one side of the storm anchor, let go the main anchor – almost certainly with a rope warp backing its chain – and drop back onto both anchors so that the angle between them is about 30° (see Fig 1.11). If you are expecting the wind to veer, this second anchor should be laid towards the direction from which the wind is expected. Again, this will double the holding power.

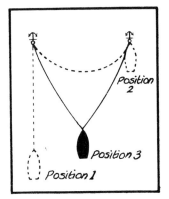

Fig 1.11 Lying to two anchors: method 2. Always lay the second anchor in the direction from which the wind is likely to be blowing if a change is expected. The ideal angle between the anchor cables is 30° although this is not easy to achieve. At that angle the holding power is double that of one anchor but it decreases as the angle increases. If the engine is not working or you do not have one, you can move from position 1 to position 2 by backing the jib. If all else fails, use method one or set the second anchor using the dinghy

Laying a Second Anchor from a Dinghy

Normally you won't have to take a dinghy to lay a second anchor, but there are times when it is the only way. Never, ever, try to load the anchor into the dinghy and go off pulling the cable. The drag will become so great that you will soon make no progress and you will tend to destroy much of the dinghy's buoyancy. Flake the required cable into the dinghy first and let it pay out as you row away.

Secondly, never stand up and throw the anchor overboard. You will probably end up joining it! Attach a short length of rope to the anchor, hang it over the stern and make fast with the rope to a thwart or other strong point using a slippery hitch (see Fig 1.12). When all the cable has been pulled out of the dinghy, release the hitch and the anchor is laid – easily and safely.

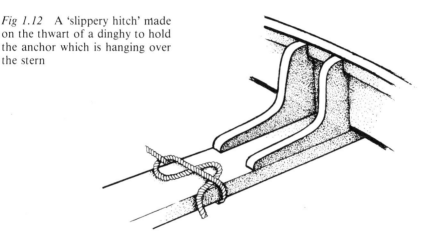

Fig 1.12 A 'slippery hitch' made on the thwart of a dinghy to hold the anchor which is hanging over the stern

After Anchoring

We are at anchor. The sails are stowed and the kettle is on. Before we go below to enjoy a well-earned cuppa, there are a few jobs we must do.

The appropriate anchor shape (a ball or ball shape made from two round pieces of wood slotted together) and, if it is dark, the anchor light, have to be rigged on the forestay. I say 'and' rather than 'or', because there is always the risk of oversleeping and, whilst it matters not if your anchor light is burning in daylight, it does matter if you are not showing the right signal. Many people are very lax and do not bother but it is important to indicate that you are likely to require a larger swinging circle than would be the case if you were moored. It is your fault if someone anchors too close to you if you haven't bothered to show the right signal – as it is your fault if you are rammed in the dark because you have failed to display an anchor light.

Now take two bearings on objects which will be easy to see both at night and during the daytime. Note the bearings in the log and a description of the objects chosen. If, later, you think your anchor has dragged, you can check using these bearings – which is why they are entered in the log and not on the back of the shopping list which will be lost when needed.

If you are staying long and are using rope cable, wrap some rag or a piece of light rope around the cable where it passes through fairleads or is in contact with anything that may cause chafe. I keep a couple of pieces of plastic tube cut with a spiral cut to slip over the rope.

Now look ashore and see if any local is trying to attract your attention. If so, go and make contact – he may know something you don't.

Lastly, go back and check that the cable is properly secured. It usually is, but . . .

Choosing the Right Equipment

The cruising ground you intend to cover will be a factor to take into consideration when choosing equipment. Unless you will be over rock for much of the time, the storm and main anchors should be chosen from the one of the ranges of patent anchors.

Stowage is also a factor to consider. Some modern boats have anchor-wells designed for a specific anchor. This is fine if the well will take the right size and right type but annoying if it is too small. If you are stuck with an anchor-well designed to take a plough of the right weight for the main anchor, you will probably choose a Danforth type for the storm anchor as it will stow flat. If, on the other hand, the well will take a plough of storm anchor size, your main anchor will be a Danforth for the same reason. The Bruce anchor fits well on the stem fitting of some boats but presents problems on others – such as those with bowsprits.

Naturally, price is a consideration. However, this is not an area where you should try to save money, as anybody who has spent a night anchored off a lee shore trying to fix the engine will tell you. The most important guide is the Lloyds Approval – always ask if you can have the anchor you are considering Certified. This usually costs extra and I am not suggesting that you should actually have it Certified – the important thing is that the supplier is prepared to make the arrangements!

I carry the following on my 40ft ketch, but I must admit that my choice was influenced by the gear already on board. The storm anchor is a Danforth type (new) and the main anchor a CQR (already there). The kedge is a fisherman, but I intend to purchase a Bruce and stow the fisherman below for use on rock only as I like the idea of a kedge which will hold in mud better than the fisherman, simply because we seem to find ourselves over mud more often than any other bottom.

Table 1.4   Some Recommended Sizes of Anchors

Boat LOA (ft)	Anchor duty	Fisherman Wt(lb)	CQR Wt(lb)	Danforth Wt(lb)	Bruce Wt(lb)
	Kedge	15	5	5	2.2
15	Main	30	15	10	4.4
	Storm	45	15	15	11
	Kedge	20	5	5	4.4
20	Main	40	15	15	11
	Storm	60	20	22	16.5
	Kedge	25	10	10	11
25	Main	50	20	22	16.5
	Storm	75	25	30	22
	Kedge	30	10	10	11
30	Main	60	25	22	16.5
	Storm	90	35	30	33
	Kedge	40	15	15	16.5
40	Main	80	45	45	33
	Storm	120	60	60	44

Notes:
The smallest drop-forged CQR anchor manufactured by Simpson-Lawrence is the 15lb. Their 5lb and 10lb anchors are cast and therefore not considered suited for duties other than as a kedge.

2
Anchor Handling and Stowing

From the point of view of sheer, physical hard work there are few jobs on board that compete with weighing the anchor, bringing it aboard and stowing it. In fact, many authorities state that the way to determine the size of boat that can be handled by a given crew is to start with the weight of ground tackle with which that crew can cope.

Since it is a heavy job in all but the smallest of boats, it is often tackled by two members of the crew working together. However, it is most important that at least two members of the crew are able to carry out the entire job – and carry it out safely – when working alone. You never know when one or the other may be temporarily indisposed. In the case of the usual family crew this means that both the skipper and his wife must be able to manage and, since it will be the wife who has the lesser strength, the system will have to be designed around her. This is not to say that she should be sent forward to carry out this task as a matter of course. Far from it, there are few sights guaranteed to annoy a male chauvinist such as myself as to see a hefty man standing near-idle at the helm while a slip of a girl is sent forward to haul on chains and anchors. Nevertheless, the day may well come when said hefty male has had an accident or is unwell and then such chauvinism must go by the board.

The first essential is a suitable bow roller over which the anchor chain runs. This must be large enough for the chain employed and the cheek pieces must be high enough to ensure that the chain will not jump off the roller. To this end, some bow-roller fittings have cheeks curved inwards (see Plate 2.1). Incidentally, when looking for bow rollers in a chandler's catalogue, they are usually to be found under the heading 'Stem Fittings'.

Some bow rollers incorporate a ratchet or pawl which locks into the links of the chain as it is hauled aboard, allowing the person pulling to relax and have a breather. It looks like a good idea but I must confess that I have never used one and I suspect that it may not work all that well in practice.

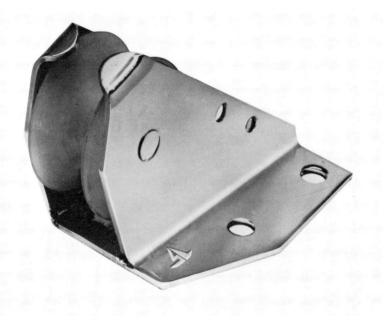

Plate 2.1 Bow roller with curved cheeks; it is most important that the bow roller or stemhead fitting is large enough. The curved tips to the cheeks help to hold the cable in place (*Simpson-Lawrence*)

Anchor Winches

On all but the smallest cruising boats, an anchor winch will be required. Although it may not be wanted for much of the time, it should be fitted unless the second strongest member of the crew can handle the heaviest anchor in complete safety – even when tired – without any aid. As always, the important words are 'in complete safety'.

Electrically operated winches, either with the motor incorporated in the winch or with an external unit driving a hydraulic pump which, in turn, drives a hydraulic motor in the winch, demand the least effort. They are, of course, expensive and they obviously consume considerable power from the batteries. Few hydraulically operated winches find their way onto cruising boats, being designed for commercial requirements. Those who normally use sails rather than the auxiliary engine may well feel that the power consumption is an overriding disadvantage and will opt for manual operation.

However, if an electrically operated winch is selected, there are a few points to consider before placing an order. It is vital that the design includes for hand operation for use when power is not available and that this works well. Some electric winches have only token emergency gear which is, to be blunt, useless. It is not difficult to

Plate 2.2 (*left*) Electric winch with remote-control switch, a very sensible and inexpensive extra, which enables the operator to move well forward to see over the bow. Even so, as the girl demonstrates, it is important to keep an eye on the winch to check that the chain is feeding onto it correctly (*Simpson-Lawrence*); *Plate 2.3* (*right*) Typical lever-operated winch. A well-sited one can enable even quite young members of the crew to haul in the anchor when conditions are favourable. I would prefer to see the young man wearing a safety harness to stop him going over the side rather than a lifejacket to save him if he does (*Simpson-Lawrence*)

include a remote-control switch unit which enables the operator to move forward and have a clear view over the bow (see Plate 2.2). This extra (indeed, this standard feature on some units) is not an expensive one and can be very useful, depending on the location of the winch. A number of winches include two-speed gear boxes. These enable the winch to haul in fairly rapidly whilst the load is limited and to change to a lower gear giving more power when required. The best winches make this change automatically as the pull required reaches a preset figure. Apart from giving additional power when it is needed, these also reduce the drain on the battery as they are operated for shorter periods than their fixed-speed cousins. Even so, the battery drain will be considerable – most electric winches consume in excess of 40 amps when the pull is about 100lb.

Hand-operated winches come with two methods of operation – a crank handle which is turned round and round (see Plate 2.4), or a

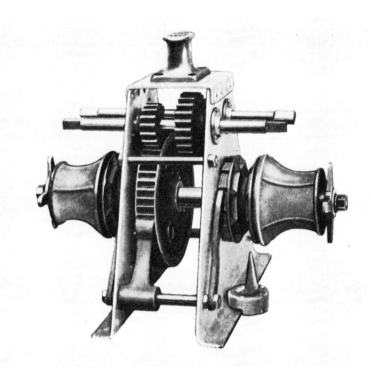

Plate 2.4 Typical crank-operated winch intended for larger craft; the rotary windlass with its two gypsies neatly solves the problem of two anchors. Greater power is obtained by using the further of the spindles which introduces an additional gear. Two people can work the windlass at the same time if required (*Simpson-Lawrence*)

lever which is pulled backwards and forwards (see Plate 2.3). The latter is easier to use on a small foredeck as the body can be wedged and one hand used to hold on while the other operates the lever. Crank handles are more suited to larger boats where there is ample space to stand up. These are usually fitted with shafts that can take two handles so that two people can operate the winch at the same time. Both crank and lever winches can be obtained with two-speed gears. Certainly this is well worthwhile when considering a lever-operated winch as it is tiring to work the lever even when there is little load; which is why most winches of this type haul in chain on both strokes, a feature that should be insisted upon.

Gypsies and Drums

The gypsy is machined so that the links of the chain fit into it. It follows that the gypsy and chain must match each other; if they do not, the chain will fit for a number of links and then slip out, which is not only annoying but can be dangerous. When ordering a winch and chain, order both at the same time and from the same supplier specifying that they are to match. If ordering a winch to handle an existing chain, cut off at least twelve links from the end of the chain and send this to the supplier so that a good match can be achieved. Most suppliers are only too happy to oblige (after all, they want you to be happy with your winch so that you will recommend it to your friends) but if for any reason the chosen supplier suggests that he does not need your sample, order your winch elsewhere. Life is somewhat harder when ordering chain to fit an existing winch. The easiest way is to order it from the winch supplier quoting the winch details and, if possible, the date of purchase. If this cannot be done, ask the supplier to let you have a twelve-link sample so that you can offer it to the winch gypsy and check that it fits. As so often in life, if in doubt – don't!

Some gypsies are designed to handle both rope and chain. If, as suggested in Chapter 1, your main anchor is fitted with both, this is the best type of gypsy to choose. Try to order the winch before the rope because each gypsy will accept only one size of rope even though it will take a number of sizes of chain.

All winches should include a rope drum as well as the chain gypsy. There will come a time when the winch will be pressed into service to carry out some other job apart from weighing the anchor. Obvious examples include hauling on the kedge following running aground and hauling on warps when working the boat from one berth to another using the time-honoured but now under-utilised method of warping.

Hauling the Anchor Aboard

All the anchor winch can do is to bring the anchor so that it is hanging up and down at the bow roller or stem fitting. The next job is to bring it aboard without damage to either paintwork or crew. Again, the need for gear will depend on the weight of the anchor and the strength of the crew. Few cruising boats carry special gear but there are a number of things that can be rigged to make life easier if one is having difficulties.

If the anchor has been fitted with a tripping line and buoy, this line should be strong enough to take the weight of the anchor. The buoy will be bobbing around somewhere and should be brought aboard first – hook the boathook around the tripping line by the anchor and haul away. Many folk use one of the halliards to pull up the tripping line and anchor but this really needs two people on the foredeck: one to pull and the other to guide the anchor aboard. However, if a short pole can be fixed to the mast with a snatch block at its outer end (a spinnaker pole?) the tripping line can be taken through the block and

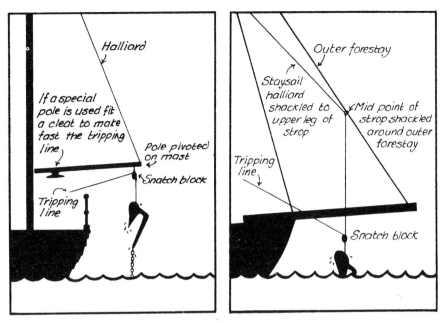

Fig 2.1 (left) Using a pole to assist in bringing aboard the anchor. (A snatch block is fitted with an opening cheek so that the tripping line can be slotted into it); *Fig 2.2 (right)* Using a block on the forestay to assist in bringing in the anchor. Method: (1) Position gear as shown and haul in on tripping line as far as possible. (2) Haul on halliard. Anchor lifts and comes inboard. (3) Continue hauling on halliard and paying out on tripping line and lower anchor on foredeck

the end of the pole attached to a halliard (see Fig 2.1). First, veer sufficient anchor cable to allow freedom of movement, haul the anchor to the end of the pole and make fast. Now haul away on the halliard and the anchor will be lifted clear of the guardrails, swing the pole inboard and lower away handsomely until the anchor is on the deck. The exact details will depend on a number of factors, and trial and error may be required to make the system work satisfactorily.

An alternative system is to shackle a snatch block to the end of one of the halliards, trapping one of the shrouds or the forestay in the shackle. Pass the tripping line through the snatch block and haul away on the halliard until the block is a few feet above the guardrails. Haul in on the tripping line and let go on the chain until the anchor is hanging on the tripping line and the anchor will then come up, blunt end first, until it is high enough to be brought in over the guardrails, lowered away onto the deck and stowed.

On my own boat, since I have a bowsprit, I use the outer forestay. However, since it is inconvenient to scramble out to fix the shackle around it, there is a length of line, roughly twice the length of the bowsprit, with a shackle seized to the mid-point which goes around the stay. There is a snatch block on one end to take the tripping line and a hard-eye on the other which is, in fact, shackled to the staysail halliard as the jib is of the roller furling type and so its halliard is not usually available. Fig 2.2 shows this gear in operation.

The point is that the human being is at a great mechanical disadvantage when leaning over the side of the boat or over the bow trying to lift even quite modest weights aboard – especially when the object is an awkward shape and likely to do damage if carelessly handled. A little thought and some fairly simple gear can make a great deal of difference. Usually mechanical advantage is not really needed, it being enough to arrange matters so that the weight can be taken with a straight back and a decent place to stand. It is worth remembering that there is no law that states that the anchor must come aboard over the bow, it is often more convenient to bring it in further aft.

Stowage of Anchors

Anchors are notoriously the most difficult of objects to stow neatly so that they are out of the way and do not become the perfect mantrap when one is working on the foredeck. As already mentioned, some modern boats include an anchor-well which is ideal so long as it is big enough (see Plate 2.5). However, the problem is not to stow just one anchor but, ideally, three.

Plate 2.5   An anchor well is fine if it is big enough. This picture raises two questions. What would happen to that tangled warp if the anchor were needed in a hurry? Since there is no samson post, are those cleats strong enough to hold the boat when things are a bit rough?

Plate 2.6 (left) Danforth anchor fitted to pulpit; *Plate 2.7 (right)* This CQR is fixed to the bow roller where a pin fits through a hole in the shank and onto a special fitting with a similar fixing. At sea, the cross bar is lashed back to the pulpit to stop the ploughshare swinging about

The working anchor must be stowed on the foredeck where it is ready for use. Some anchors stow very neatly on the bow roller (see Plate 2.7), which is excellent so long as the fastenings are secure. Others stow on chocks on the foredeck, which is acceptable so long as they are in the right place. It cannot be taken as read that the anchor will be in the best place; it is just this sort of error of detail which can spoil otherwise excellently designed and built boats. If there is the possibility that a better place can be found, lay the anchor in various places and then try out the usual foredeck jobs such as kneeling to change headsails and working at the mast until the best location is found. Plate 2.6 shows a Danforth anchor stowed on a pulpit. This is a neat and tidy arrangement for the smaller boat which will not be out at sea overmuch – the strain on the pulpit would be considerable if there were seas breaking over the bow.

The kedge is best stowed aft. There are two reasons for this: it is the lightest anchor to move around the place and, in the event of running aground, this is where it will be wanted. The first attempt at refloating is usually either to take the kedge away in the dinghy or to

Plate 2.8 Bruce anchor stowed on special-purpose bow fitting. These anchors will stow satisfactorily on a number of standard bow fittings

fling it as far as possible (depending on its weight) back along the track and to try to haul the boat off the way it came on. Incidentally, if anchoring for a short spell, there is no reason why the kedge should not be let go from aft so long as the warp has been taken forward outside everything first. If there is room aft of the cockpit, it can be stowed on chocks there; if not, space will have to be found in one of the cockpit lockers.

It is the storm anchor that presents the greatest problem. By definition it is heavy and will be needed when conditions are such that the motion of the boat will make moving it around difficult. Either it will be stowed on the foredeck to add to the general clutter or it will be stowed below. The choice will depend on the available space on the foredeck and on the difficulties involved in bringing it on deck. A compromise is to fit suitable chocks on the foredeck but to keep it below, bringing it up onto deck if it looks as though it may be required but before life becomes too trying. In this case, it must be remembered that the first job after lashing it down in its chocks is to shackle on the cable!

Stowing Anchor Chains

The basic requirements of stowage were dealt with in the previous chapter. However, if three anchors are carried there may well be a problem – two anchor chains and only one chain pipe! There are ways and means of overcoming this without creating a second chain pipe but, in the long run, such schemes result in far more effort. If the anchors are light enough to be handled without a winch, there is no real difficulty. If a winch is used, however, the second chain pipe has to be positioned just aft of the chain pipe incorporated in the winch so that as much chain as possible is held on the gypsy when hauling in. In some cases, the angle of attack between the gypsy and the after chain pipe can be improved by mounting the winch on a plinth of timber.

When fitting a winch to a boat which was not designed to include one, it is usually impossible to locate the winch so that it is both in the right place to make operation as easy as possible and directly over the existing chain locker. If so, jt is well worthwhile trying to make a new locker. If this is not possible, a wooden slide in the shape of a shallow 'U' can be used to help guide the chain as required, but it must be wide enough to ensure that the chain cannot jam. In any event, it is always good practice to have a crew member below flaking down the chain neatly so that it can be let go in a hurry without worrying about it.

Being heavy, ground tackle must be stowed with an eye on the trim of the boat. Chain should be kept as low as possible and it may be that it has to be stowed further aft than is convenient to avoid the boat becoming too bow heavy. Such matters can be determined only by trial and error and many skippers find that it can take two or three seasons of experimenting before they are really happy with the trim of the boat. The whole matter becomes even more complicated if the boat is used for both day sailing and cruising as the extra stores carried when cruising also affect the issue.

3

Mooring, Berthing, Warping and Slow-speed Working

There are a number of occasions when we need to be able to control the boat very precisely at slow speed – when picking up a mooring, berthing alongside a quay or pontoon, making our way through a crowded anchorage or rescuing a member of the crew who has fallen over the side to name the most usual. Given slack water and little or no wind, such manoeuvres present no problems. Life, however, becomes increasingly complicated as these two natural forces build up. The reason is that the slower the boat is moving, the greater the influence of the wind and the tide until there comes a point where these two natural forces are affecting the boat more than the sails or the engine.

It is, therefore, important to be able to judge the speed and direction of both wind and water and to know just how the boat will be affected by them at various speeds on various courses. This takes a great deal of time and a great deal of practice – there are so many variables involved that there is no alternative to experience although much can be done to speed up the learning process.

Nine times out of ten, the approved method of stopping a boat is to turn her head into the tide. It is, of course, possible to use the engine running astern as a brake and we will look at that later. However, the surest and safest method is to use the tide. Under some conditions the wind will have the greater effect and it is then necessary to turn into the wind rather than the tide – again, only experience can provide the judgement needed to decide which course of action to take. A good exercise is to spend time observing the swirl of water around fixed objects – moored craft, mooring buoys, piles etc – and to turn the boat's head into the tide and cut the engine. Compare the distance travelled until the boat stops (stops over the ground, not through the water) with the 'look' of the water. Repeat the exercise at various speeds. Before long, especially if the wind is calm when trying out these exercises, it will be possible to judge fairly accurately how far the boat will carry her way against the tide and so to judge when to turn into the tide to stop at a given point – a mooring buoy, for example. Although it makes sense to try out a new boat in a deliberate fashion, this process of 'learning the feel' of the boat should never cease and a good helmsman is always observing the water and noting the effect it is having on the boat under his control.

Exactly the same comments apply to the wind. Indeed, many shallow-draught craft with high topsides will be affected to a greater extent by the wind than by the tide. By choosing slack water, similar experiments can be carried out but this time the helmsman will be watching the burgee and noting the feel of the wind instead of watching the water.

Gradually, and it is a gradual process, the helmsman will find that he is automatically gauging the power of the natural forces and can use them as friends rather than as difficulties to be overcome. The process can be speeded up by taking all way off the boat and letting her drift. When lying in the water with no power applied, most boats will turn their bows away from the wind while the stern turns into the wind. A point of balance will be achieved and the boat will then be pushed bodily through the water. It is very useful to know how quickly the boat takes up her 'natural attitude', what that natural attitude, is and at what speed she will then drift. Obviously, the relationship between the tide and the wind will affect both the natural attitude and the speed of drift. Again, thanks to the endless possibilities, it takes a great deal of experience to be able to judge accurately just what will happen.

Unfortunately, almost nothing amuses seagoing folk with time on their hands as much as leaning on a wall and watching the visitors in their boats. Their cup of happiness runs over when they can witness the antics of an inexpert crew trying to pick up a mooring buoy or berth alongside a quay. It follows, therefore, that these evolutions must be carried out in a quiet and seamanlike fashion. This may sound a touch facetious. Far from it. It is at just such moments when the skipper and his crew – and especially the skipper – are feeling embarrassed that tempers flare, voices are raised and stupid accidents happen. The fear of looking a fool is responsible for as many mistakes as any other cause and the only cure is to know the boat – a cure that requires time, training and a good deal of experience.

Picking Up Mooring Buoys

The usual method employed when picking up a mooring buoy is to send a hand to the foredeck armed with a boathook whose job it is to hook onto the buoy, bring it aboard and make fast the mooring chain (or make fast to the buoy in certain cases). There is nothing basically wrong with this method provided that the boat can be held stationary while the foredeckhand carries out this duty. Sadly, what tends to happen is that the foredeckhand hooks on perfectly satisfactorily and then finds that the weight of the boat comes onto the boathook and he is forced to pull the buoy aboard and make fast while holding the boat in position. Apart from being very hard work – especially when the foredeck is manned by the skipper's lady wife as so often seems to be the case – this is dangerous. A crowded mooring is not the place to lose a crew member over the side, especially when the boat is drifting out of control.

The secret is in those words 'hold the boat stationary'. If we are using the engine (and this is probable as, in this day of crowded harbours, there is rarely room to manoeuvre safely under sail) it is rare that the natural conditions will make it impossible to hold the boat stationary over the ground for quite long periods. Again, it is a question of practice. When tide and wind are together, there is no real problem. By approaching the buoy from down wind and down tide and gradually throttling back, a state of balance can be achieved. The same applies when the wind is in direct opposition to the tide. The problems occur when the wind is at an angle to the tide. If, for example, the wind is on the beam, as soon as the boat ceases to make way through the water and, indeed, for some time before that – the wind will tend to blow the bows away. Under these conditions, it can be very difficult to hold the boat stationary although near-balance can be achieved with experience. Luckily, total balance is not required. All that matters is that the boat be held in place long enough for the mooring to be made secure which, if the foredeck-hand is good at his job, is not for long. However, if the mooring is not secured in time, it is generally safer to let everything go and circle around for a further try than to leave the foredeckhand hanging on.

The trouble with talking about boats working at slow speed is that everything has to be hedged about with words such as 'probably' and 'generally' simply because different boats behave differently in similar conditions and the same boat can behave very differently when subjected to a strong tide and a weak wind as opposed to strong wind and weak tide. Although it is usually safer to abort a mooring attempt rather than continue with it, there are some exceptions, the main one being when there is a powerful wind backing up a strong tide and the boat is somewhat under-powered. In these cases, the boat can be swept away out of control long before the power available can create steerage. If there are other craft moored nearby or some other obstruction, such a move can spell disaster. It is all a question of knowing the boat. Fortunately, few small cruisers are so under-powered as to fall into this category except those fitted with an outboard motor far smaller than that specified by the builder. Much larger sailing craft with auxiliary engines are more likely to be difficult to handle under engine in these circumstances but are usually crewed by experienced seamen.

There are a number of special spring clips available on the market which make the job of connecting with the mooring quicker and simpler. These usually fit onto the boathook or include a similar pole. The idea is that the foredeckhand simply hooks onto the buoy and withdraws the boathook, leaving the boat attached by the clip and a short length of line. These clips work very well when the mooring buoy is shackled directly to the mooring chain (see Fig 3.1) and incorporates a strong ring. With the type of mooring which uses a buoy attached to the chain with a rope riser (see Fig 3.2), this system should not be used unless it is known that the rope riser is strong enough to take the weight and is in good condition.

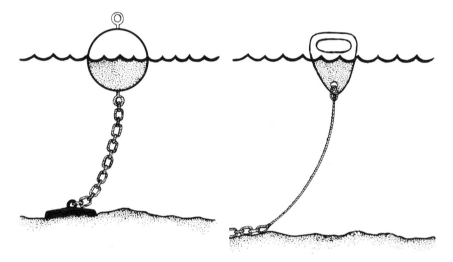

Fig 3.1 (*left*)   Mooring buoy attached directly to mooring chain; *Fig 3.2* (*right*) Mooring buoy attached to mooring chain with rope riser

Although requiring more cumbersome gear, a system whereby all the work can be carried out from the safety of the cockpit is worthy of consideration. For this a warp is required long enough to run from the cockpit up to the bow fitting through fairleads and then back again, but outside everything (see Fig 3.3). The end is fitted with a large snap-shackle so that it can be clipped onto the buoy ring, if fitted, or onto the mooring chain itself. Instead of aiming to stop the boat with the buoy under the bow, the buoy is brought alongside the cockpit. Since the coamings at this point are usually low, it may be possible to dispense with the boathook altogether or, failing that, to use a much shorter one than usual. As the boat comes up to the buoy the latter is picked up by one of the crew and the snap-shackle is made fast as required. There is bound to be a certain amount of slack in the mooring chain and so the boat need not be stationary but can be allowed to forge ahead very slowly until the shackle is secured.

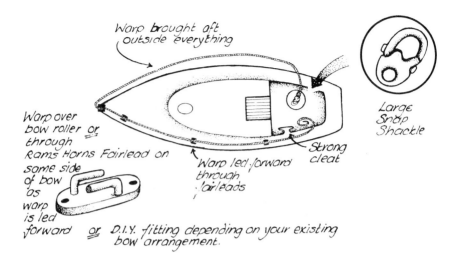

Warp brought aft outside everything

Warp over
bow roller or
through
Rams Horns Fairlead on
some side
of bow
as
warp
is led
forward   or   D.I.Y. fitting depending on your existing
bow arrangement.

Warp led forward
through
fairleads

Strong
cleat

Large
Snap
Shackle

Fig 3.3   Arrangement for mooring from the cockpit

The engine is put into neutral and, as the boat falls back, the warp is hauled in. When the snap-shackle comes up to the bow fitting, the warp is made off on a strong cleat in the cockpit and all is secure until there is time to go forward and make fast as usual.

There are three advantages to this system. Firstly, it overcomes the difficulty that many boats are so designed that the helmsman, being unable to see through the bows, loses sight of the buoy whilst it is still some distance away and must rely on a signal from the foredeckhand to bring the boat over the buoy. Secondly, since they are close together there is good and easy communication between the helmsman and the crew member making fast. This makes life far easier, especially if it is decided to abort the attempt and try again. Lastly, no single member of the crew has to hold the weight of the boat on his own. If the boat falls back very quickly and before the warp is hauled home, there are two people in the cockpit to put their weight on it. In view of the fact that the final work on the foredeck can be done at leisure, two crew members can go forward to carry out that work if conditions – such as a very strong tidal flow – warrant such a precaution. The disadvantages are the need to carry extra gear and to rig up a suitable arrangement on the bow.

Mooring under Sail
In the event of engine failure or in an open and uncluttered mooring, the decision may be taken to moor under sail. This is not as difficult as some people suggest but, like any other manoeuvre, it does call for some degree of training.

Once again, the aim is to stop the boat at the mooring buoy and to hold it there long enough to make secure. It is far easier when there is ample wind available to provide power and is best not attempted if the wind is so light that it is difficult to make any way against the tide – unless the crew is sufficiently experienced to make a 'running moor'. This last involves, to put it simply, sailing past the buoy at whatever angle can be achieved, making secure very quickly and being prepared to drag down the sails even when full of wind with similar rapidity. Since, by definition, there will be little wind, this is not impossible; it does, however, demand rapid and precise work by all involved. The main risk is that someone will get hurt due to the boom swinging etc, rather than that there will be risk to gear or boat. The reason I stress the risks is that I once saw a small child knocked over the side as the mainsail gybed during just such an evolution. Everyone on board was too busy to notice; everyone else (myself included) was too far away to help in time. Apparently the child had been told to stay in the cabin but had come up into the cockpit regardless – and without a life jacket. Although there was a fair tide running, it was a beautiful and calm day. Tragedy can strike when least expected.

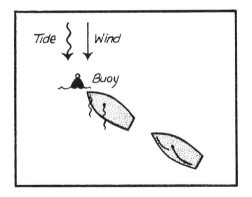

Fig 3.4 Mooring to a buoy against wind and tide

So, let us assume there is ample wind and that it is blowing in the same direction as the tide. The approach is made, close hauled, at 45° to wind and tide (see Fig 3.4). As the boat closes with the buoy, the sheets are started and wind spilled in exactly the same way as the throttle is closed when using the engine. As soon as contact is made with the buoy, the headsails are let fly and the mainsail used to provide enough push to hold the boat steady for a few seconds. Time will be limited and all should be ready to abort the effort and to turn down wind and try again.

Fig 3.5 shows the safest approach when the wind is against the tide. Again, practice is required to be able to run a boat up into the tide so that it stops as required. Once stopped, the helmsman loses all control and the buoy must be secured quickly – all being prepared to go round and try again if the attempt fails.

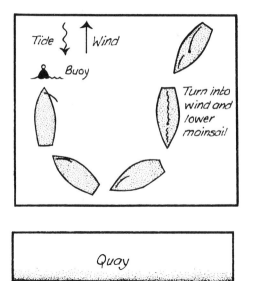

Fig 3.5 Mooring to a buoy with wind against tide

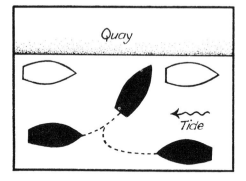

Fig 3.6 Berthing alongside a wall against the tide

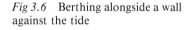

Fig 3.7 Berthing alongside a wall against the tide between two other vessels

When the wind is across the tide the helmsman has the choice of approaching under jib, down wind and turning up onto the buoy or of approaching close hauled and sailing up to the buoy. The choice will depend on the angle the wind is making to the tide and on the type of hull and the strength of tide. This raises the question of what will happen to the boat when attached to the buoy with the sails set. If the hull has a deep keel, the tide is strong and the wind less so then the boat will probably swing to the tide regardless. If this means that the sails will fill and she starts to sail away making it difficult to hand the main – the approach should be made under headsails only if at all possible. If, on the other hand, she will settle head to the wind – either because of or despite the tide – the approach can be made with all sails set.

Berthing Against a Quay

Under ideal circumstances, the objective is to stop the boat a foot or so away from and parallel to the quay or wall. If the tide is running along the wall and there is little wind, this can be achieved by turning into the tide as shown in Fig 3.6. This assumes, however, that there are no craft moored alongside which will hamper the approach. So often, thanks to the popularity of cruising, it becomes a case of working into a small space and a different approach becomes necessary.

Assuming that there is either little wind or that it is blowing with the tide, the approach can be made at 45° (see Fig 3.7) and the bow taken in tight to the wall. A crewmember then steps ashore with a warp and makes fast on some suitable point then the tide is used to swing the stern into position. Clearly, it is essential that helmsman and crewmember work as a team and this means that the situation should be considered carefully before the attempt is made. If necessary, make a couple of slow passes before berthing, agree just where the boat is going to be taken in and how the crewmember will make the quay – a ladder or mooring ring might be available, or you might be lucky and the levels right for a simple step ashore. Also agree where the first warp is to be made fast and how far back the boat is to be allowed to drift. The more carefully the manoeuvre is planned, the better the chance of bringing it off without any problems.

If the wind is blowing onto the quay, the boat can be brought to a halt as shown in Fig 3.8 and allowed to drift into position. The odds

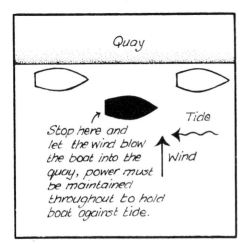

Quay

Tide

Stop here and let the wind blow the boat into the quay, power must be maintained throughout to hold boat against tide.

Wind

Fig 3.8 Berthing alongside a wall when the wind is blowing onto the wall

are that the bow will drift in first and a crewmember can then step ashore with a warp or hook on with a boathook. This may not be essential, but it soothes the nerves of the skippers of the boats either side to see an attachment made as soon as possible.

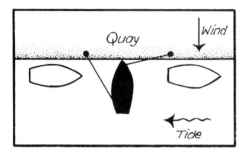

Fig 3.9   Berthing alongside a wall when the wind is blowing off the wall. Ideally the crewmember going ashore should take both warps but the head rope should be made fast first – and taken up against the tide. The faster the tide is flowing, the further towards the flow the approach should be

The most difficult situation is when the wind is blowing off the quay. In such a case the approach is best made at right angles to the wall as shown in Fig 3.9. Again, a couple of passes to plan the action and to ensure that everyone knows exactly what has to be done will pay dividends. Once the bow is attached, the boat can be allowed to fall into position if the tide is strong enough but it will almost certainly be necessary to use a stern warp and pull the boat in. This warp is passed from the stern forward outside everything and thrown ashore so that the crewmember there can make it fast to a suitable point. It is usually better to pull from the boat rather than the quay so that the spare warp is aboard rather than cluttering up the quayside.

Making Fast
Before looking at the question of the lines needed to ensure the security and safety of the craft, it is worth considering a simple piece of equipment often used by ferryboats. They spend a great deal of

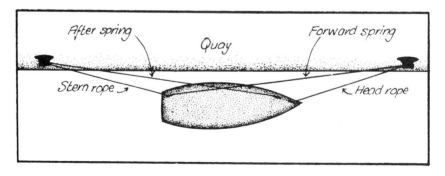

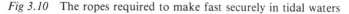

Fig 3.10   The ropes required to make fast securely in tidal waters

time lying alongside but not tied up and they use a short length of warp with an eye splice in one end and a piece of thick, round rod bent into a hook at the other. This is hooked through a ring or dropped over a bollard and cleated off as a temporary measure while embarking and disembarking passengers. A couple of these are very useful pieces of equipment as they do make it easier and quicker to make the first contact with the shore.

However, having arrived and made fast in a temporary way, we need to hold the boat in close to the wall and stop it from surging forwards and backwards. At the same time, all lines must be long enough so that they do not become taut at low tide. This can be achieved by using four lines as shown in Fig 3.10. The bow and stern lines will stop the boat from drifting away from the quay but will not stop her from surging. This is the job of the springs which, by virtue of their length, will be affected far less by the rise and fall of the tide. These must be long – as good a length as any is twice the LOA (length overall) of the boat. Table 3.1 shows sizes of suitable warps against LOA. It is always better to err on the heavy side rather than to skimp on warps.

Table 3.1   **Suitable Rope Diameters for Warps**

Boat Size (ft)	Polyester: Braided (mm)	Polyester: 3-strand (mm)	Polypropylene (mm)	Nylon (mm)
18	12	12	12	10
22	14	14	14	12
28	16	16	18	14
34/40	18	20	22	16

Notes Warps must be strong enough to hold the boat in the worst possible berth (an exposed position) since the time will come when it cannot be avoided. The above sizes will suit average-displacement craft; heavy-displacement craft should be fitted with heavier warps. There is much to be said for using three-strand rope so that one end of each warp and spring can be given an eyesplice.

Head and stern ropes should be at least equal to the length of the boat and preferably $1\frac{1}{2} \times$ length. Springs should be at least $2 \times$ length and preferably $3 \times$ length. Two short (2 metre) ropes fitted with eyesplices at each end are invaluable for temporary mooring and making the first contact with the shore.

Fenders

Before the boat comes anywhere near a quay or wall – and especially anywhere near another boat – there must be sufficient fenders available and in position. Few, if any, boats carry enough fenders especially as today's crowded harbours are often so full that boats must berth two or three abreast against quays and pontoons. If there is the risk that another boat may berth alongside, it is as important to fender the outboard side as that against the quay; you never know when some idiot will come up alongside and ruin the paintwork.

In general, three types of fender may be bought (see Plate 3.1). Although amply strong enough to cope with 'normal' conditions, the pneumatic types tend to burst when needed most – when they take the weight of the boat thrown against a wall as can happen during storms or when things go awry during berthing. Cheaper and more effective are old tyres. These, however, do not look as well nor are they as easy to stow. Even so, it pays dividends to find space for at least two or three even if a full complement of 'bought' fenders is carried.

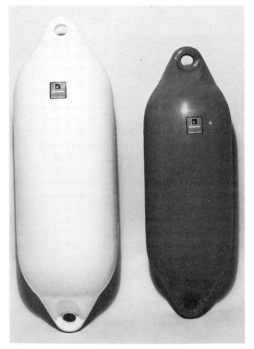

Plate 3.1 Typical fenders. This type may be hung either vertically or horizontally (*South Western Marine Factors*)

If tyres are used, try to obtain the smaller sizes without wire reinforcement. Drill (brace and bit), hack (old chisel – keep the first-aid kit handy) or saw (hacksaw) three holes or slots about 2.5cm (1in) square. Two of these should be about 13 or 15cm (5 or 6in) apart, the third on the opposite side. These are all cut through the face of the tyre and a length of rope is eyespliced through the top two, the third acting as a drainage hole. It is short-sighted to use old rope; it will break and not only is the fender lost but the boat is then exposed to damage which can cost a great deal more to repair than a length of new rope. The rope should be over long – at least long enough for the tyre to be below the water line from the highest part of the deck with sufficient left over to make it fast. Avoid the temptation to take a short cut and splice this rope around the tyre, it will chafe away in no time. If you are worried about the tyre leaving black marks on the topsides (a very real worry), this can be avoided either by finishing the tyre off by wrapping old rope around it or by making a suitable canvas bag (see Fig 3.11). These bags are bound to wear fairly quickly but are cheap and easy to make.

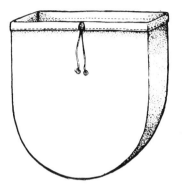

Fig 3.11 Tyre fender in a canvas bag. Bags can be made from any tough material – old tarpaulins and sails are ideal. The drawstring is pulled tight around the rope attached to the tyre

In an emergency, old plastic water containers (the 2½ gallon size is best), sailbags stuffed with clothing or bunk cushions held in a 'network' of cord can be pressed into service. If consideration has been given to these possibilities, the necessary bits and pieces can be prepared and stowed away in the 'emergency store'.

Putting out fenders is usually a straightforward job, the exception being when berthed against an uneven surface such as a wall with piles. There are two ways of overcoming this problem. The easiest is to hang the fenders in the usual way and then to rig a plank or spar outside them to work against the piles or whatever. The problem is

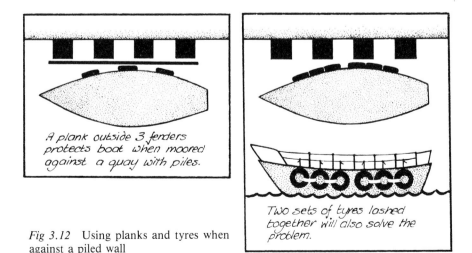

A plank outside 3 fenders protects boat when moored against a quay with piles.

Two sets of tyres lashed together will also solve the problem.

Fig 3.12 Using planks and tyres when against a piled wall

that there is rarely stowage space for a suitable plank. The second method is to hang a series of tyres over the side and to tie them together so as to form a solid fender of sufficient length to ensure protection. The two methods are shown in Fig 3.12. At least six tyres are needed for even a modest-sized boat and six tyres demand a fair amount of stowage space. All in all, the biggest problem is that of stowage and it is regrettable that more space is not 'designed into' many modern boats. The reason is, of course, that the poor boat designer is forced into trying to get a quart into a pint pot!

The Gentle Art of Warping

Every now and then, it is obvious that the boat cannot be positioned as required using normal techniques. Then is the time to use the art of warping – an art that may or may not involve the use of an anchor as well. Consider the problem of berthing in a very tight space with a strong tide and wind pushing the boat onto the quay. Clearly, normal methods would result in, at best, a nasty bump when the boat hits the wall. Instead, an anchor can be dropped some way from the wall – with a tripping line and buoy – the ground is bound to be foul and the anchor will have to be retrieved at an angle so will have to be weighed using a longer line attached to the tripping line. Once the boat has swung to the anchor, the cable is let go slowly so that her stern drops in towards the wall. As the stern nears the quay, a line is sent ashore and made fast. Hauling on this line as the anchor cable is let go will pull the stern around so that the boat will drop neatly into place.

The same technique can be used to warp a boat out of a tight spot, although in this case the anchor will have to be laid using the dinghy.

Some boats just will not behave themselves when going astern and it is most helpful to be able to turn them round so that they can leave a berth with the engine ahead. The same technique can be used to ease a boat out of a berth where she is hemmed in both ahead and astern by other craft. Examples are shown in Figs 3.13 and 3.14.

Engines at Slow Speed

Most screws turn in a clockwise direction when viewed from astern and the boat is going ahead. This means that there is a tendency for the stern to be dragged to starboard because the bottom of the screw is operating in deeper, and therefore denser, water than the top. This effect is most noticeable when turning a boat around as she will turn with a smaller turning circle to port than to starboard (see Fig 3.15). The reverse applies when the engine is put astern – the stern tending to move to port.

In many situations this effect is a nuisance but it can be used to

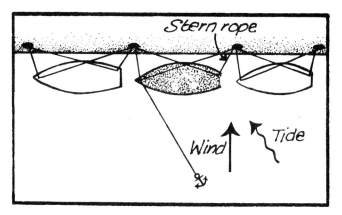

Fig 3.13 Hauling away from a tight berth. (1) Lay out anchor using dinghy in the general direction of the tide. (2) Double stern rope. Cast off all other lines (this will stop her inching up with the tide). (3) Haul in on anchor rope whilst paying out stern rope (carefully fending off). (4) Start engine – slow ahead. (5) Drop stern rope and weigh anchor

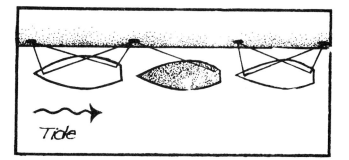

Fig 3.14 Leaving a tight berth using warps
(a) Let go all ropes except stern spring which is doubled. Push off bow and tide will swing bow out. Engine ahead as boat reaches about 45° with wall. Cast off spring taking care to keep it clear of propeller. (Bow spring would be used if tide was in opposite direction)

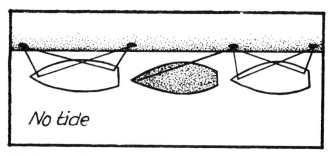

(b) Let go all ropes except bow spring which is doubled. Engine ahead with starboard helm – stern swings out. Engine astern and cast off spring

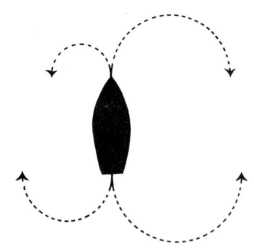

Fig 3.15 With a righthanded propeller (ie clockwise when going ahead) a boat will turn tightly to port and less tightly to starboard. Astern the effect is similar but some boats refuse to turn against the propeller effect. Lefthanded propellers reverse the above

good effect when berthing as a touch ahead or astern will kick the stern to one side or the other without causing significant fore and aft movement. It is worth bearing in mind that a boat pivots around a point some way forward of mid-point so kicking the stern over will also swing the bow in the opposite direction. If, for example, the boat has stopped more or less as planned beside a quay but a touch too far away from it for the crewmember on the foredeck to go ashore, kicking the stern out can have the effect of pushing the bow in just far enough. Like so many of the evolutions mentioned, it is a technique that should not be used unless it has been practised first in open water so that the helmsman knows exactly what will happen, how much throttle is needed and what, if any, helm to apply.

If a boat is moving slowly and a change of direction is required, it is best to give a short but hard burst of power rather than a longer but lesser burst. This is because the swirl of water created alongside the rudder will have a definite effect, whereas a slow application of power will merely gradually increase speed and considerable forward movement will result before there is an appreciable turning movement. This, of course, assumes that the screw is on the centre line and forward of the rudder. Those with wing engines cannot use this technique. If the auxiliary is an outboard, even if it is usually fixed and the rudder used for steering, it can be very useful if it can be pivoted for slow-speed work.

Anchors Aweigh
It sometimes happens, especially in a strange and crowded port, that you just have to stop in a hurry and there is not sufficient power in the engine to stop in time even when full speed astern. A typical case occurred some years ago in the river Dart when a boat was approaching the Higher Ferry blissfully unaware of the fact that this ferry

operates on the floating-bridge principle with two wire hawsers stretched across the river which guide it from side to side. Too late the skipper realised that he was about to be trapped in front of the floating bridge between the cables – not that he was to be the first nor, doubtless, the last. Fortunately he always took the precaution of rigging the kedge over the stern with the cable made off to a suitable length. A quick slash with a knife and the kedge tumbled into the water and the boat was brought up short a few feet from trouble.

If you follow this system you will have to put up with the leg pulling and mirth of your friends but one day you might decide it was all well worth while.

The Drive Method

Before leaving this subject, we might as well take a brief look at what can be described as the drive method. Driving can be achieved only when using the engine. The boat is driven towards the target at a fair speed and, at the last moment, the engines are put hard astern to stop her where required. This is very spectacular. It calls for accurate action, split-second timing and gear that will behave exactly as required. The only advantage (other than showing off) is that by keeping the speed up the effect of wind and tide is somewhat reduced. However, I still blush with shame whenever I recall a certain day when I was using this technique in a 65ft motor vessel I then owned. My justification was that she carried a lot of tophamper and was hard to control at slow speeds if there was much wind about. At the critical moment, the reversing gear jammed and we rammed the wall at some 4 knots – more than fast enough in a boat weighing over 20 tons! I turned to a friend standing beside me and apologised. 'Don't apologise to me,' he said, 'It's your pride that's hurt, not mine.' From that day to this I have never used the drive method – the cost can be far too high when things go wrong.

4
Pilotage
and Basic Navigation

Pilotage can be defined as 'the conduct of a ship in the neighbourhood of danger'. Such dangers include the coast when close, narrow waterways, rocks, shoals, harbours and so forth.

Navigation is more general being defined as 'the science which enables a ship to be conducted from point A to point B in safety'. This is achieved by maintaining a record of the ship's movements and by taking observations of terrestrial and celestial objects so as to determine the ship's position from time to time.

Pilotage

From the above definition it follows that the seaman who is piloting his ship is usually in close visual contact with the land. There is, therefore, a close relationship between pilotage and normal map reading. Both skills demand that objects on the ground can be identified on the map or chart and that symbols on the map or chart can be used both to identify objects on the ground and to build up an accurate mental picture of the area. In both cases the action required – or the course to be followed – is determined, in the main, using visual judgements unaided by instruments. It is, therefore, of paramount importance that the pilot has a thorough and precise knowledge of the meaning of all symbols used on charts and a list of these, together with abbreviations, is shown in *The Macmillan & Silk Cut Nautical Almanac.*

Despite the broad similarity between map reading and pilotage, the sailor faces one important factor which he will not find on land. All the time his ship is moving relative to the water, that water is moving relative to the land. This applies to both the pilot and the navigator and is dealt with more fully later in this chapter. However, the mental picture of the area must include a mental picture of the water movement within that area.

Those who sail regularly in a given area soon know it very well and utilise that knowledge – often on a subconscious level – to use the various tidal flows and wind patterns created by local land masses so as to exploit them to the maximum. Clearly, a cruising man visiting an area for the first time cannot have this intimate knowledge. He can, and should, learn as much as possible from all available sources of information – charts, pilots, maps (which often show landmarks omitted on charts) etc. Not only will this care help to ensure the safety of the ship it will enable the pilot to make the best possible use of all the available natural forces.

Since it is assumed that all readers have some experience of sailing and boatmanship, to labour the obvious points regarding ship handling in confined waterways would be tedious. However, a couple of comments may not be out of place based on the time-honoured motto of the scouting movement – 'Be prepared'. At all times know how to stop the ship if necessary and always plan an escape route. This means thinking ahead.

To elaborate on these thoughts: you are entering the harbour entrance shown in Fig 4.1. You have both tide and wind against you but the wind is strong enough to enable you to tack against the ebb. There is a freighter following you but there should be ample time to reach the safety of the inner wall before she catches up with you. You are busy demonstrating your skill to those on the wall watching

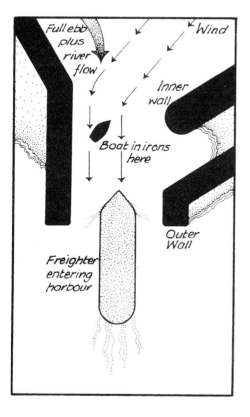

Fig 4.1 Illustration of boat in harbour mouth referred to in text

when, without warning, as you tack at the point shown in the sketch the wind changes direction and you are in irons. The ebb starts to pull you back and, suddenly (as always when things go wrong), the freighter seems very close, very fast and very big. What are you going to do?

If you back the jib to port you will swing out in front of the freighter, if you back it to starboard you will probably hit the wall. The sails flap loudly, driving all sensible thought from your head. The boat drifts ever faster towards the freighter.

What we did (yes, I regret it is a true story) was this. The chap on the foredeck who had prepared the anchor and cable ready for use looked over his shoulder, let out a loud yell and threw the lot overboard. This somewhat restricted the choice of action open to the skipper and, by the time everyone had realised what had happened, the freighter was steaming by at a safe, but too small for comfort, distance.

In fact it was bad seamanship to have been there in the first place. Having seen the freighter approaching, we should have either motorsailed in quickly or waited outside and followed her in. We should, if we were intent on sailing in, have discussed and decided on a course of action in the event of finding ourselves in irons. It is possible we would have decided to anchor as we did, but it was also bad seamanship to have had no contingency plan. I repeat, 'Think ahead and keep thinking ahead'. That way you will have a plan when things go wrong and, when that happens, active thought usually ceases.

Practise the art of stopping. Not just stopping in the water but stopping relative to the land in a variety of tidal flows. It is nearly always possible to stop a boat in the water but this is of no avail if the current then sweeps you into a dangerous situation. At all times you need sufficient power available, be it engine or sail, to face into the current and remain stationary relative to the ground.

Navigation

Although I have defined navigation as a science, *Reed's Almanac* describes it as an art (one suspects that Captain Watts himself wrote the passage). Both words are right: and both words are wrong. The navigator uses scientific principles but the information he uses is determined by his judgement – and judgement is the meat of art. I mention this now because it is very important to remember that a line drawn on a chart is no more than a line drawn on a chart. It may reflect the results of the navigator's scientific calculation based on his artful judgements and it may represent the ship's track (or whatever) but it remains a line. The worst mistake a navigator can make is to assume that his workings and plottings are truly accurate. He should suspect everything until he has definite proof – and even then he should remain a touch sceptical. The wrecks littering the coasts of the world bear mute witness to the truth of this.

As far as the coastal cruising navigator is concerned, he uses his skills for three purposes:

1   To plan a passage so that it may be made safely and so as to use the winds and tides to the maximum advantage (which applies whether using sail or engine).
2   To keep as accurate a record as possible of the ship's track so that its present position is known at all times.
3   To confirm the second purpose by establishing the ship's position as often as possible using any means available.

Before looking at these in detail, we must discuss the various means by which we describe the ship's position, its course and the movement of the water beneath us.

The prime instrument carried on board every boat is the magnetic compass. For the time being we will assume that this always points to the north and south poles (it doesn't but we will look at that later). The circle around the compass is divided into 360 degrees (360°) with the 000° pointing to the north. A compass rose is shown in Fig 4.2. The compass may carry other notations as well and some navigators use these instead of the 'three-figure or circular notation' as shown in the figure. I highly recommend that these other notations are ignored and that the navigator uses the three-figure system as it is simpler to understand and less likely to cause errors.

The magnetic compass enables us to describe the direction of one object from another (eg the ship from a shore mark or one shore mark from another) and the direction in which the ship is heading, the course she is following and the direction in which the water is flowing. Above the compass rose in Fig 4.2 is a ship heading on a bearing of 060° (not 60°; we shall see why later), which means that the 060 mark on the compass rose is in line with a mark on the compass bowl which is in line with the ship's centre line; this mark is called the Lubber Line. An observer looking over the compass at the lighthouse would see the line marked 310 lining up with the light-house which is said to be on a bearing of 310°. The tide is flowing in the direction of 115°.

So much for direction, we also need to be able to measure distance and speed. Distance is measured in nautical miles which are, for all practical purposes, 6,080ft as opposed to land miles of 5,280ft. Speed is measured in nautical miles per hour known as 'knots'. We do not speak of knots per hour as this would mean nautical miles per hour per hour (which is meaningless unless, I suppose, one is thinking in terms of acceleration). The name 'knot' comes from the old method of measuring speed. A shaped piece of wood (the log) attached to a long line with knots tied into it at intervals was thrown over the stern. The number of knots pulled out in a given time, usually a minute, indicated the speed of the ship. To this day, we call instruments for measuring speed or distance run 'logs'.

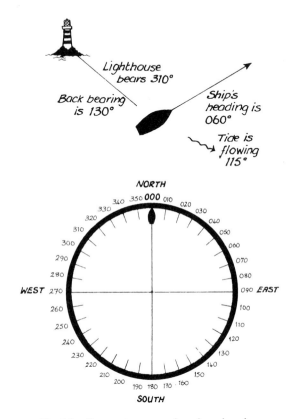

Fig 4.2   Compass rose and various bearings

We can now define the ship's course as being on a given bearing at a given speed; its position by means of two bearings of objects ashore (each bearing providing a 'position line' along which the ship must lie, its position being at the point where these two position lines cross) or by the bearing of one object and the distance between that object and the ship. The movement of the water can be defined in the same way as the ship's course, by a bearing and a speed.

With these three measurements plus time we can describe everything we need to describe and plot everything we need to plot on the chart.

Water Movement

The time has come to take a closer look at this question. We can plot the track of a ship on the chart by drawing a line on the chart on the same bearing as the ship's steered course and of a length which represents the distance travelled in the period under consideration. Naturally, this line should start from the point on the chart which represents the point from which the ship started on the ground. However, during that period the water will have been moving relative to the ground and so the ship will not end up at the point represented by the end of the line we plotted. Before we can make the correction required to compensate for this water movement, we have to be able to assess the direction and speed of the flow that has been affecting us.

Table 4.1   Tidal-flow Table for Points Marked on Fig 4.4

	HOURS	A		B		C	
		Dir^n.	Rate (Kn)	Dir^n.	Rate (Kn)	Dir^n.	Rate (Kn)
AFTER HW WESTHAVEN	6	059	1.1–0.5	105	1.4–0.8	057	1.0–0.5
	5	067	1.4–0.7	101	2.8–1.4	074	2.1–1.0
	4	074	1.5–0.7	101	3.6–1.8	078	2.9–1.4
	3	081	1.3–0.6	108	3.7–1.8	074	2.8–1.4
	2	093	0.6–0.3	117	2.2–1.1	081	2.0–1.0
	1	136	0.1–0.1	121	0.7–0.3	074	0.7–0.3
	HW	229	1.0–0.5	261	1.0–0.5	283	0.6–0.3
BEFORE HW WESTHAVEN	1	252	1.1–0.6	263	1.5–0.7	261	1.2–0.6
	2	265	1.6–0.8	270	2.8–1.4	258	2.5–1.2
	3	271	1.6–0.8	267	3.6–1.8	252	3.4–1.7
	4	281	1.4–0.7	261	3.0–1.5	252	3.0–1.5
	5	306	0.5–0.2	258	1.5–0.7	250	1.8–0.9
	6	029	0.4–0.2	158	0.2–0.1	296	0.5–0.3

As we shall see in the next chapter, this information is available from a number of different sources. For the moment we will consider one of the ways the information is presented on charts. If you look at Fig 4.4, which is a very simple chart, you will see three points marked A, B and C, the letters being in diamond shapes. These are points for which tidal information is available and it is given as shown in Table 4.1; this table is usually printed on the chart itself. As you would expect, the information is given in the form of a bearing and a speed. However, against each hour of the tidal cycle there is not just one speed but two (headed in some tables as springs and neaps). The faster rate applies during spring tides and the lower during neaps so the navigator has to estimate the probable rate after consulting the tide tables and checking the height of the appropriate tide. The tidal information shown is based on the time of high water (HW) at the reference port – Westhaven – and so we need to find the range (ie the amount the tide rises or falls) at that port for spring tides as well as on the day in question. With these to hand we can assess the rate as it will apply. We look at the tide tables and find that HWMS (high water mean springs) has a height of 3.6m and LWMS (low water mean springs) one of 0.2m. Later we shall see how these heights are derived, for the moment we are interested only in the range which is HWMS minus LWMS or 3.6–0.2 or 3.4m. By a similar calculation we determine that the present range is 2.0m. To find the actual rate, we multiply rate shown for springs by that present range and divide by the spring range. Thus, if the rate shown under springs is 2.8 knots, the actual rate to apply would be $2.8 \times 2.0 \div 3.4$ which is 1.6 knots. This does not give an exact answer but is accurate enough for our purposes.

Using this technique we find that the tide is running at a dead 3.0 knots on a bearing of 090°. We are steaming at 5 knots. What will be the effect of this tide on the ship as it follows various courses?

Steaming into the Current   Our course is 270° and so the flow is directly against us. Our direction will not be altered but we will set back by 3 miles in the next hour. We are steaming at 5 knots and so will make only 2 miles over the ground.

Steaming with the Current   Our course is 090°, with the flow. As above, our direction will not be altered but this time we will be carried 3 miles by the flow and so will make 8 miles over the ground. These figures are not unusual and show how important it is to work the tides when the rate of flow is in the same order of magnitude as the speed of the ship.

Steaming at an angle to the Current   It rarely happens that the ship is heading either directly into or against the flow. In all cases when the course and flow are at an angle to each other, we must plot both on the chart to determine the effect of the tide.

Plotting the Ship's Track

For this exercise we need the four main tools of our trade: a pencil (2B is best as it can be rubbed out easily), a rubber, a pair of dividers and a pair of parallel rules. Various types of parallel ruler are available, but I find the old-fashioned type with two sections held by two links which one 'walks' across the chart is the easiest type to use in a small boat – the ones with rollers tend to slip no matter how careful one is – and I have a Captain Field's Pattern with degrees marked on it. This is a boon when working on a small chart table as you don't need to use one of the compass roses printed on the chart – you read the bearings off the ruler against any line of longitude (the north-south lines). Apart from being able to fold the chart as you want instead of having to include a compass rose, this reduces the movement of the ruler over the chart which, in turn, reduces the risk of it slipping. I suggest that you use graph paper for the various exercises – the type with the larger squares divided into tenths.

Consider Fig 4.3. If you look at the top left-hand plot first, this is the plot of a ship steering a course of 000° at a speed of 5 knots. We mark the starting point with a dot in a circle and the notation FIX1000. This means that that was our position at 1000 hours (how we fixed our position we will come to later). From that point we draw a line on the same bearing as the course steered, in this case 000°, and we mark off the distance made good in the time, 5 nautical miles as we are steaming at 5 knots and considering one hour. At the end of the line we write DR1100 which means that this is our 'dead reckoning' at 1100 hours. The dead reckoning is the probable position of the ship ignoring all water movement. We put one arrowhead on the line and write the course steered beside it using three figures. This tells us that the line represents a course steered and we write the bearing beside it just in case we have to check that the plot was correctly carried out.

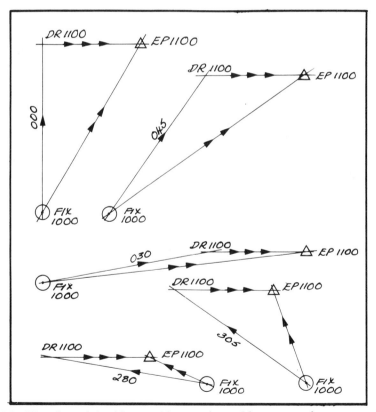

Fig 4.3 The effect of the tide on a ship steaming at 5 knots on various courses. The tide is setting on a bearing of 090° at a rate of 3 knots

Already we have defined some of the notations we are going to use on the chart and it is absolutely vital that we know what each notation means and that we always use it to mean the same thing. By the end of a passage, the chart can be covered in lines and it becomes very confusing unless each one is clearly identified. Any three-figure number is a bearing, any four-figure number is a time, any line marked with a single arrowhead is either a course steered or a course to steer. Incidentally, on longer passages some people use a 'date time group' instead of just the time. This creates a six-figure number, 071100 being 1100 hours on the 7th of the month. If you do use this, I suggest you write it 07/1100 to remind you which two figures represent the date (110011, for example, can be confusing).

Having found the DR, we draw a further line to represent the tidal flow for the time in question, in this case a line at 090° marked off to represent 3 miles as the flow rate was 3 knots. We draw a triangle around the end of that line and add EP1100 – our 'estimated position' at 1100 hours, ie the probable position of the ship after taking into consideration tidal flow. This line is marked with three arrowheads to indicate that it represents the movement of the water. Finally, we complete the triangle and mark that line with two arrowheads. This line represents the ship's track although, as we shall see later, the actual track is rarely on this line but is an arc of a circle lying close to the track as plotted.

The other examples are plotted in the same way: course steered–tidal flow–ship's track.

Planning a Passage
This is a subject that is given little attention, certainly far less than it deserves. Care taken in planning a passage can ensure that the skipper is alerted to any dangers en route and that they can be avoided as well as enabling the maximum advantage to be taken of the tidal flow. Another advantage of passage planning is that it enables the skipper to set watches so that the more experienced members of the crew (often the skipper himself) are on watch at critical times such as when nearing the coast or making an important course change. The point behind this comment is that it often happens that the skipper of a small and fairly experienced crew takes great care to ensure that the crew rests but fails to ensure that he gets enough rest himself. If he is working to a passage plan he knows in advance when he will be able to go below and, indeed, may make this a requirement when deciding on the plan. I do not believe that small boats with small crews are the right ships on which to set regular watches. It is far better to tailor the watch-keeping rota to each passage and sometimes to arrange for watch changes on the basis of distance run rather than time. Naturally, larger craft or those with

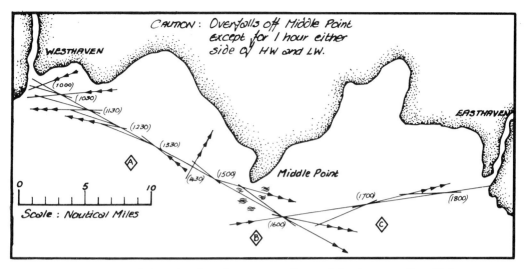

Fig 4.4 Chart used for planning the passage discussed in the text. For tidal information see Tables 4.1 and 4.2

crews of considerable experience will stick to the usual 4- or 3-hour watches.

To return to the subject in hand, consider the chart shown in Fig 4.4. We are moored some 5 miles up the river at Westhaven and are to sail to another mooring about 5 miles up the river at Easthaven. Tides are at springs and HW at Westhaven will be 0830 and 2100; HW at Easthaven is an hour later at 0930 and 2200 and we expect it to be rather dark at 2200. The forecast suggests a steady south-westerly wind which will enable us to maintain a steady speed of 4 knots. What is the best time to leave our mooring at Westhaven, assuming we wish to make a day voyage?

Let us look at the main factors we have to take into consideration:

1   We shall need an ebb tide to help us down the river at Westhaven.
2   We shall need a flood tide to help us up the river at Easthaven.
3   We must pass Middle Point during slack water, ie one hour either side of either HW or LW, to avoid the overfalls.
4   We have never been to Easthaven before and want to arrive with some daylight in hand.

As it will take us about an hour to reach the entrance at Westhaven after we slip our mooring, we can leave at any time between high water and one hour before low water. This can be stated as from HW to five hours after HW (HW + 5), in this case from 0830 to 1330. Likewise, we want to arrive at the entrance at Easthaven during the period from LW to one hour before HW to allow an hour for the trip up the river. This can be written as from HW − 6 (roughly LW) to HW − 1. As HW Easthaven is an hour after HW Westhaven this means from 1600 to 2100. Even if we arrive at the end of this time zone, we shall have an hour of daylight in hand.

Obviously, the only slack water available to us at Middle Point is either side of LW in the middle of the day. LW at Middle Point will be about half an hour later than LW Westhaven which is at 1430. We must pass the point between 1400 and 1600.

Ignoring the effect of the tides for a moment, it will take us about four hours to sail from the entrance at Westhaven to Middle Point – probably a bit longer as the tide will be against us – and the same time to reach Easthaven entrance from Middle Point. Let us plan to arrive at Middle Point at 1400 so that we can afford to run a bit behind schedule (it is always possible to waste time but never possible to make it up). That would mean leaving our mooring five hours earlier at 0900, which is within the time zone by half an hour, and we should arrive at Easthaven entrance four hours later at 1800, well within our time zone there. Now we must plot that decision on the chart to make sure it works and prepare our course table. First, however, we must look at the method employed to plot a 'course to steer'.

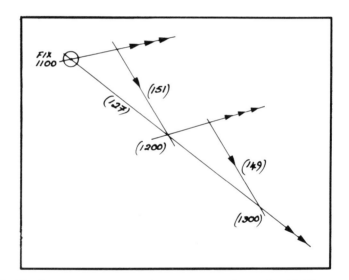

Fig 4.5   Plotting a course to steer: plot course to make good – tidal flow – course to steer

This is similar to the method shown in Fig 4.3 except that we plot everything in the reverse order. If you remember we found the ship's track by plotting the course steered – tidal flow – ship's track. To find the course to steer we plot course to make good – tidal flow – course to steer. Consider Fig 4.5. We wish to follow a course of 127°. The tidal-flow table informs us that the tide will be setting on a bearing of 078° at a rate of 2.9 knots for the first hour and 074° at 2.7 knots for the next hour. We anticipate being able to make a speed of 6 knots through the water.

First we draw a line to represent the course to make good. Some say that this should be marked by two arrowheads but, although I have marked such lines in some of the figures I prefer to leave these blank when I am working on a chart as they are the only ones not marked, which identifies them absolutely from a line representing the ship's track. However, it is a good idea to mark the bearing and put it in brackets as this saves working it out again. Next we draw a line to represent the tidal flow for the first hour, 078°, and use the dividers to mark the distance it will have run, 2.9 miles. This is the position to which the ship would drift, assuming that the tidal prediction is correct and there is no wind, during that hour. However, we shall be making 6 knots. Set the dividers at the distance representing 6 miles, place one point on the end of the line representing the tidal flow and swing the other point around until it meets the line representing the course to make good. Draw a line through these two points and measure the bearing which may be written, again in brackets, alongside. This is the course to steer for that hour. Lastly, mark the tidal-flow line with three arrowheads, the course-to-steer line with one and note the time you expect to be back on course, still in brackets. Repeat the exercise for each hour.

Although we have slightly muddled our notations by using the same arrowhead codes for planning as we did for plotting the track, this should not cause confusion. For one thing, all times and bearings which relate to planning have been put in brackets and, for another, as we plot the track we shall be rubbing out the plan.

Let us now return to our proposed voyage from Westhaven to Easthaven. We are now ready to plot our plan and to prepare our course table. The plan has been plotted on Fig 4.4. The scale is too small to show all the notation but it confirms the main points we were

Table 4.2 Course Table for Passage Planned in Fig 4.4

Time	HW±	Interval	Tide Point	Dir^n.	Rate	Course to Steer
1000	+1	½hr	A	252	0.6	106
1030	+2	1hr	A	265	1.6	101
1130	+3	1hr	A	271	1.6	108
1230	+4	1hr	A	281	1.4	117
1330	+5	1hr	A	306	0.5	121
1430	+6	½hr	A	029	0.2	129
1500	−6	1hr	B	105	1.6	125
1600	−5	1hr	B	101	2.8	079
1700	−4	1hr	C	078	2.9	088

Note: Tidal rate for intervals other than 1 hour is adjusted as required

worried about as it shows us passing Middle Point between 1500 and
1600 (perhaps a little later than we would have liked but still safe) and
arriving a couple of miles off Easthaven at 1800 with ample time in
hand. As we drew this plot, we prepared our course table (Table 4.2);
this is fairly self-explanatory and, if part of it seems unnecessary,
such a procedure helps to cut down errors. From the table you will
see that there are two intervals of half an hour instead of an hour.
The first was used to bring the intervals in line with the time of HW
(ie 30 minutes past the hour) simply because this makes it easier to
plot the tidal-flow information. The second was used because the
influence of the tide as predicted at point A was judged to cease at
1500 hours as point B was approached. As it happened, this also
coincided with the time when we ceased to think in terms of the

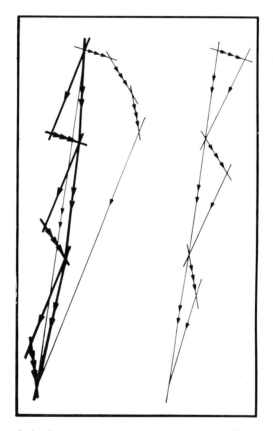

Fig 4.6 Effect of plotting a course to steer over a number of hours. On the left the
course has been planned by plotting 3 hours of tidal flow and one course to steer.
The thick lines represent the plot of the ship's track showing that it bows from the
theoretical track. On the right is a plot based on intervals of one hour. Although the
ship will be nearer the theoretical track it will not quite make the same distance in the
3hr period

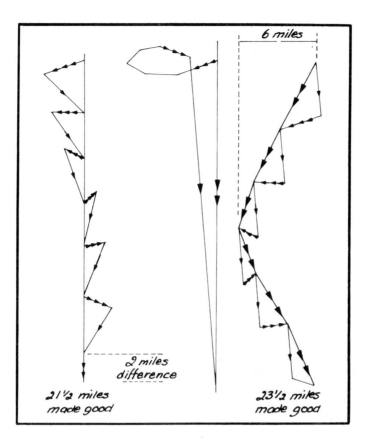

Fig 4.7 A comparison between plotting using six 1hr intervals and one 6hr interval

morning HW plus and turned to the evening HW minus. The other point to note is that a course table of this type is of no use unless we start off in the right place. This starting point, known as the 'point of departure', should be a fix. When leaving a port it is usually possible to obtain a good fix using three bearings. As soon as this fix is obtained it should be plotted on the chart and, if it is significantly different from the point of departure used on the plan, the course for the first interval should be recalculated so as to bring the ship back to the required point at the end of that interval. This question of fixing the ship's position is considered in a later section.

Before leaving planning, it should be noted that the interval can be extended as there is no absolute need to work in hourly intervals. Fig 4.6 shows how an interval of 3 hours can be plotted. As can be seen, the actual ship's track will bow towards the direction in which the tide is flowing. The longer the interval, the further the actual track tends to be from the theoretical track. However, plotting on an hourly interval basis, whilst it keeps the ship nearer the theoretical track, does not necessarily mean that it will achieve an increase in the distance run as shown in the right-hand plot.

This is demonstrated in Fig 4.7 where a plot covering six 1-hour intervals is compared with one covering a single 6-hour period. As can be seen, the latter plot increases the distance made good during the 6 hours by 2 miles. However, beware of this system if there are any dangers anywhere near the theoretical course line. To the right is the plot of the ship's track and it is 6 miles away from the theoretical track in one place. If using a long-interval plot when there is any risk of approaching danger, plot the track as shown in the figure to ensure that the proposed course is safe (this can be done on a piece of tracing paper laid on the chart to avoid piling confusion on top of confusion).

There is, however, one time when it is advisable to plan a passage with an interval greater than an hour. If the navigator wishes to go below for a few hours, he will sleep more soundly if he has been able to give the helmsman a single course so eliminating the risk of a course change being made at the wrong time or onto the wrong course.

So much for planning the passage; now we must look at the role of the navigator when the ship is at sea.

Recording the Ship's Track

Up to now – for the sake of simplicity – we have ignored both the effects of leeway and the fact that our compass does not point to true north. We already know how to record the ship's track. The plot should be brought up to date at intervals of no more than 4 hours – more often when near the coast or other danger – using the method we used in Fig 4.3. In other words, we plot the course steered to find the DR, the set of the tide to find the EP, and add the line representing the ship's track. Obviously, the basic information required to enable the navigator to maintain his plot must be kept. This should be recorded in the deck log, which we will look at later, by the duty watch. This log notes every course change, the ship's speed or the distance run (noted every half hour) as well as any other factor that will help to maintain the plot or establish the ship's position. This log is vital – without it the navigator is lost (in more senses than one) – and the skipper must ensure that all members of the crew are aware of the need to keep accurate records at accurate intervals.

Leeway We must now rectify one of our omissions, the effect of leeway. As we all know, unless a ship is running with the wind, the actual course through the water will be different to the ship's heading thanks to leeway. Incidentally, this applies to boats when under power as well as when sailing. A centreboard boat can make as much leeway when under power with the plate up as she does when sailing with it down.

Luckily there is a very simple way to solve this problem. The

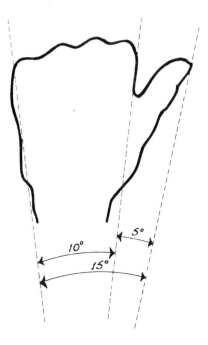

Fig 4.8 The natural angles of the hand. Form a fist as shown and hold the hand at arm's length. Note that the thumb is held in a relaxed position and not stretched. The angles shown are fairly usual but check your own 'natural angles' with the compass

navigator gives the helmsman the course to steer – say 150° – and then lets him make the allowance required. To do this, the helmsman settles the ship on the given course and looks aft at the wake. This will be making an angle with the fore and aft line of the ship. Using either the compass or the hand's natural angles (see Fig 4.8) the helmsman judges this angle, let us assume it is 5°, and turns the ship up into the wind by that amount. He then notes both the course steered, in this case 150°, and the ship's heading, either 145° or 155° depending on which tack the ship is sailing, in the deck log. It may be, of course, that he is unable to hold the course required as it is too close to the wind. In this case he notes the ship's heading on the best course he can hold and, after estimating the leeway, the course steered. It is not always easy to judge leeway but the helmsman is in the best position to make the estimate and must do his best. Incidentally, in my experience leeway is usually under-estimated rather than the reverse, possibly owing to wishful thinking.

Compass Error We have also omitted to take into account compass error, the difference between the direction in which the compass points and a true bearing as it would appear drawn on a chart. It is caused by two factors, magnetic variation and compass deviation.

The compass points to magnetic north and the magnetic pole is not situated at the North Pole (the same applies at the south magnetic pole). It is, in fact, in northern Canada and is not static but rotates around a point, each rotation taking about a thousand years. The effect of this is that the difference between magnetic north and true north varies depending on whereabouts on the earth's surface one is and also, but by a very small amount, from time to time. The amount by which it differs is called *magnetic variation* and each compass rose printed on charts carries details thus: 'Var^n 7° 45' W(1969) decreasing about 6' annually'. However, if you consult special charts which indicate the geographical differences in variation by lines joining together all points with the same variation – 'magnetic variation charts' and printed in almanacs such as *Reed's* – you will find that the total difference in variation throughout the British Isles is 2°. This is so small that it can be ignored for all practical purposes.

The second factor is called *compass deviation* and is caused by the effect of the ship's own magnetic field on the compass. Even a boat made of wood has enough metal in it to create a magnetic field and often this is altered when certain electrical circuits are used, a point we shall come back to later. As the ship changes her heading, so this field rotates and changes its effect on the compass. It is essential that this compass deviation is known for every heading and this is determined by carrying out an operation known as 'swinging the compass'. If the following method is adopted, not only will you have the great satisfaction of being able to swing your own compass but the operation will give you the total compass error – thus killing two birds with one stone.

For this we need a piece of equipment called a pelorus (see Fig 4.9). In essence this comprises a compass rose divided into 360° which is fixed to the ship so that the 000°–180° line is parallel to the ship's fore and aft line. Mounted over this is a sighting pointer so that we can take a bearing of an object outside the ship and read off an angle which describes that object relative to the ship's heading. Fortunately, it is very easy to make a pelorus and details will be found in the next chapter.

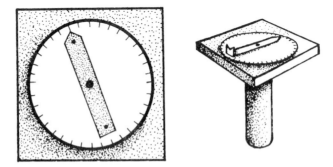

Fig 4.9   The pelorus consists of a pointer with sights swinging over a compass rose – fixed so that the 000° to 180° line is on or parallel to the ship's fore and aft line. It is used to measure the angle between the ship's fore and aft line and an imaginary line drawn from the ship to an object outside the ship

In addition to the pelorus we want a calm day, good visibility, slack water, someone to man the pelorus, a good helmsman and a known transit. A transit is an imaginary line drawn through two objects which can be positively identified on the chart. By drawing a line through these objects on the chart we can measure the bearing of the transit very accurately. We are going to drive the ship over this transit line on a variety of different compass courses and measure, using the pelorus, the angle between the transit line and the ship's fore and aft line. We can then calculate the true heading of the ship, compare it with the reading on the compass and so find the compass error.

Prepare a blank table as for Table 4.3 and complete column 1, the compass course to be steered. The helmsman drives the ship slowly and steadily on each course in turn so that it crosses the transit line. Meanwhile, the person on the pelorus sights along it keeping the nearest of the two objects in line with the sights, turning the pointer until both objects line up. The pointer is then held still and a reading taken which is entered in column 2 alongside the appropriate compass course. This sounds complicated but is quite simple although it does require a little practice. If the courses are taken in a logical order (eg 000°, 195°, 015°, 210° etc) the job can be completed fairly quickly. Remember, however, that the results are only as accurate as the transit chosen and that the two objects should be as far away as possible to ensure a good result. Although a transit can be one where the ship is between two objects, for this exercise they must be to one side, as otherwise it is almost impossible to operate the pelorus and judge the moment when the ship crosses the line at the same time.

Table 4.3   Table Used to Swing the Compass Using a Pelorus

Column 1	Column 2	Column 3	Column 4	Column 5	Column 6
Compass Course Steered	Pelorus Reading	Ship's Heading	Compass Error	Ship's Heading	Compass Course
000	274	351	+ 009	000	009
015	258	007	+ 008	015	023
030	241	024	+ 006	030	036
045	224	041	+ 004	045	049
060	207	058	+ 002	060	062
075	191	074	+ 001	075	076
090	175	090	nil	090	090
105	160	105	nil	105	105
120	144	121	− 001	120	119
135	129	136	− 001	135	134
150	115	150	nil	150	150

165	101	164	+001	165	166
180	087	178	+002	180	182
195	073	192	+003	195	198
210	060	205	+005	210	215
225	046	219	+006	225	231
240	033	232	+008	240	248
255	019	246	+009	255	264
270	006	259	+011	270	281
285	352	273	+012	285	297
300	337	288	+012	300	312
315	322	303	+012	315	327
330	306	319	+011	330	341
345	290	335	+010	345	355

Note: The transit bearing used in the above was 265°

Now we can go home and work out the results in front of the fire. First, determine the true bearing of the transit line from the chart. To find the ship's heading we subtract the pelorus reading from the transit bearing (adding 360 if the answer is negative); this is entered in column 3. The compass error is found by subtracting this figure from the compass course, in other words: compass course – ship's heading = compass error. Note the sign and enter the figure in column 4 (you may have to use 360 instead of 000 for the first compass reading).

Fill in column 5 using the same figures as in column 1, add these to the compass error, again note the sign, and enter the result in column 6. Make a fair copy of the table in the ship's log and don't forget to make a note of the transit bearing used. It may be wanted later.

Although this table gives us all the information we need, it is not presented in the best way. Table 4.4 shows the neatest method. The middle column of the three is filled in first showing intervals of 5° from 000 to 355. The left-hand column comes from column 3 of Table 4.3; fill in the figures available first, add 5 to each line for the line underneath and subtract 5 from each line for the line above. Repeat the exercise using column 6 for the right-hand column.

We now have a record of the compass error – ie magnetic variation and compass deviation – for the ship on all headings which will be accurate for the place in which the compass was swung and quite accurate enough for a wide cruising area. In any case, if we travel too far from home, the error is known – it is the unknown error that causes problems.

Using the table is very simple; you just follow the arrows. To convert a true bearing off the chart into a compass bearing for the helm, look up the true bearing in the middle column and move right. To convert the compass bearings noted in the deck log, be they for courses steered or for bearings taken, to true for the chartwork look up the bearing in the middle column and move left.

Table 4.4 Compass Error Table as Used on the Chart Table and by the Helmsman

TRUE ◄——— COMPASS			TRUE ◄——— COMPASS		
	TRUE ———► COMPASS			TRUE ———► COMPASS	
351	000	009	178	180	182
356	005	014	183	185	187
002	010	018	187	190	193
007	015	023	192	195	198
012	020	028	197	200	203
019	025	031	200	205	210
024	030	036	205	210	215
029	035	041	210	215	220
036	040	044	214	220	226
041	045	049	219	225	231
046	050	054	224	230	236
053	055	057	227	235	243
058	060	062	232	240	248
063	065	067	237	245	253
069	070	071	241	250	259
074	075	076	246	255	264
079	080	081	251	260	269
085	085	085	254	265	276
090	090	090	259	270	281
095	095	095	264	275	286
100	100	100	268	280	292
105	105	105	273	285	297
110	110	110	278	290	302
116	115	114	283	295	307
121	120	119	288	300	312
126	125	124	293	305	317
131	130	129	297	310	322
136	135	134	303	315	327
141	140	139	308	320	332
145	145	145	314	325	336
150	150	150	319	330	341
155	155	155	324	335	346
159	160	161	330	340	350
164	165	166	335	345	355
169	170	171	340	350	360
173	175	178	346	355	004

Ideally we need two copies of this table – one for the chart table and one by the helm. These should be glued onto a sheet of plywood and given two good coats of varnish, you may be sure they will get wet!

We have now eliminated our former simplifications – without too much hardship – and can record the ship's track on the chart using the methods described, ending up with our EP (estimated position). However, the accuracy of this plot depends on many factors and it is almost impossible to eliminate all errors. These factors include the fact that it is very difficult to sail a small boat on a given course without some deviations, especially when working to windward and trying to take advantage of any slight change in the wind; that the tidal predictions we are using are no more than predictions and local weather conditions can make a great deal of difference to both the direction and rate of flow of the tide; that we have to maintain an accurate record of our speed which may be constantly changing – which is why a distance run log is really of more value than one just showing speed although all logs are subject to problems – and that leeway has to be estimated. It follows that the track plotted should be checked as often as possible by establishing the ship's actual position whenever this can be achieved.

Establishing the Ship's Position

Although there are many ways of establishing the ship's position, including taking sights of celestial bodies, using radar and taking radio bearings, at this stage we will consider only the use of visible terrestrial objects and the depth of water below us.

The key to this aspect of navigation is the position line. A position line is a line drawn on the chart on which the ship is known to lie. The most accurate position line is a transit – a line linking two objects which can be identified on the chart. All the navigator has to do is to draw a line on the chart through those objects and he has a dead accurate position line without any calculations or other errors. The good navigator grabs every opportunity of noting a transit with both hands. As the ship passes over the transit line, the time is noted in the deck log together with the distance run as shown on the log (confusing having two totally different objects with the same name – this is the log we trail to show our speed and/or how far we have steamed) or the ship's speed depending on the type of log used.

The next most accurate position line is to take a bearing of an object and to plot that bearing line on the chart. This can be done in two ways. The hand-bearing compass will give a magnetic bearing – but is subject to deviation in the same way as the steering compass. The only difference is that we know the deviation for the steering compass and we cannot know what, if any, to allow when using a hand-bearing compass. A better method is to use the pelorus. The helmsman maintains a steady course while the pelorus reading is taken of the object. Convert the compass reading to true, using the compass error table, add in the reading on the pelorus (subtracting 360 if the result is greater than that) and you have the true bearing of the object in question ready for plotting on the chart.

Since a position line is, by definition, a line on which the ship is known to lie, if two or more position lines can be obtained at the same time, the ship must be at the point where the lines cross. Fig 4.10 shows a number of such lines. It is rare indeed that these are so

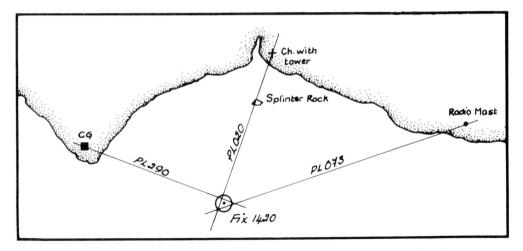

Fig 4.10 A fix obtained using 3 position lines – one is a transit. The smaller the cocked hat, the more accurate the fix. The objects chosen should be about 90° apart if possible for accuracy and certainly more than 30° and less than 150°. However, any fix is better than no fix and all position lines should be plotted

accurate that, when more than two position lines are obtained, they will all cross at the same point. The triangle formed by these three lines is known as a cocked hat – and the ship should be shown as being in the centre of the cocked hat unless there is danger nearby in which case the ship should be placed at the point of greatest risk. Establishing the position of the ship by this, or any other, means is known as a 'fix' and the notation used is a dot surrounded by a circle with the note FIX followed by the time (or date/time group if used). Personally, I like to mark my position lines so as to reduce confusion and I use the notation PL225 (where 225 is the bearing).

Once a fix has been established, this is used as a new starting point for the plot. However, the EP associated with the fix should be found and the two compared. If there is a wide difference between them something is wrong and the error should be found. It could be a simple mistake by the navigator but it might be that the compass is reading incorrectly. This could be because someone has left a metallic object near to it and this is the cause of all the trouble. Two objects often improperly stowed are winch handles and the boat-hook. A boat-hook laid along the coach-roof grab handles with its metal tip near the compass can cause chaos. Don't neglect to check below – the cook may have lodged the pressure cooker on a lee bunk just beside the compass if it is bulkhead mounted. The problem of electricity has been mentioned; if the boat is badly wired, certain circuits may affect the compass. Try switching things on and off and see whether the compass moves. If it does, have the wiring fault put right at once.

Gradually, as one becomes more experienced, the plot will become more accurate and the fixes nearer to the EP. The only way to improve is to practise and so a full plot should be kept even if the trip does not seem to warrant it; in any case, visibility may suddenly deteriorate and it is then very comforting to know where you are.

Unfortunately, it is not always possible to find two or three objects which can be identified on the chart at the same time and so we must look at other methods. Let us assume that we can only see one suitable object, as is often the case at night when the object is a light. We take a bearing of the object and note the time and the reading on the log. For the next period of time we must maintain as steady a course as possible. We then take a second bearing of the object, noting the time and the reading on the log. We choose any point along the position line of the first bearing and assume, for the moment, that that is the position of the ship at the time when the first bearing was taken. From there we plot the ship's track up to the time the second bearing was taken. If we draw a line through the EP so found which is parallel to the position line of the first bearing, we have drawn a line on which the ship's position at the time the second bearing was taken must lie – it is, in fact, another position line but we now call it a 'transferred position line' (notation, if used, should be TPL). If we now plot the position line resulting from the second bearing, it will cross the transferred position line and so fix the ship's position as at the time the second bearing was taken. This method is called the 'transferred position line method' and a fix so obtained is called a 'running fix'.

It sometimes happens, in bad or at least poor visibility, that one only manages to get a single bearing on each of two objects. The same method can be used by transferring the first position line across to meet the position line from the second object. The accuracy of this system depends on how accurate the plot is between the two bearings and there is no way in which this accuracy can be checked. However, if two position lines are transferred to cross a third, a cocked hat will be created. If this is small, the fix can be considered good – if over-large it should be treated with suspicion. This method is shown in Fig 4.11.

However, there are two times when a single position line is quite enough. We have already noticed that the ship's position can be defined by a bearing and a distance. It is usually very difficult to judge distance at sea but the one time distance can be judged accurately is when an object is either just dipping below the horizon or rising above it. Thanks to the curvature of the earth, the distance from an observer's eye to the horizon is a function of the height of that eye above sea level. Most almanacs contain tables which give you the distance of the horizon for various heights and this is a fact that every navigator should have firmly fixed in his mind. At 7ft it is, as near as makes no odds, 3 miles.

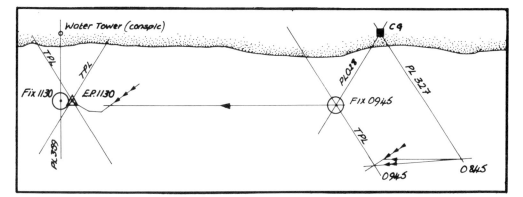

Fig 4.11 Transferred position lines. We are sailing past a coastline with few good landmarks. We manage to take two bearings of the coastguard station and obtain a running fix at 0945. It starts raining and visibility deteriorates dashing our hopes of a second running fix based on the water tower. At 1130, we see the water tower and take a bearing before losing sight of it again. We plot the position line, work up the plot to find our EP1130 (the track line has been omitted to avoid confusion), transfer the position lines used for the previous fix and create a cocked hat. It is rather large so we 'fix' at the point of greatest risk – in this case nearest our destination

However, the height of the object itself also determines when it will become visible. Again, the tables in most almanacs give the details. These give distances off for objects of various heights for observers at different heights. Whilst all this is interesting, it is very difficult to judge when an object is 'rising or dipping' as it is called unless that object happens to be a light and it is night. It is probably for that reason the almanacs title the tables 'Distances off Rising and Dipping Lights'.

To show how this can work in practice, let us assume that we are crossing a wide bay at night in good visibility (see Fig 4.12). As we near the point where we expect the first light to 'dip' – and these distances should have been worked out in advance as it is never easy to consult tables in a small boat at night – we take a bearing on the light every few minutes and, when the light finally dips, we use the last bearing taken to plot a fix. Likewise, we keep our eyes open and take a bearing of the next light as it rises to provide the second fix. Light-hopping in this way is a good and safe method of navigating so long as the track is clear of dangers and, of course, visibility is good.

The last weapon in this restricted armoury for establishing a ship's position is the echo sounder. At all times depth can be used to check a position by comparing the actual depth with that shown on the chart. If there is much local variation in depth, it is possible to use depth in conjunction with a single position line to establish a fix.

There are, of course, many other methods but the above will see the navigator through most cruises. Basically, it is the job of the navigator to make full use of every clue he can find. He should never

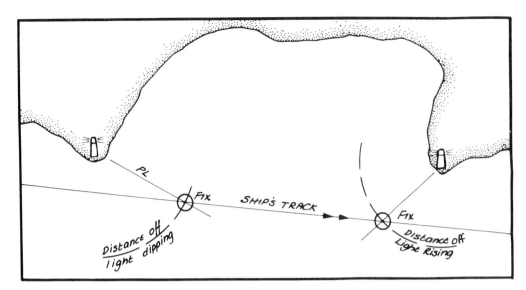

Fig 4.12 Light hopping at night: use a single bearing to provide a position line and calculate distance off as the lights rise and dip

fail to keep an accurate plot of the ship's track – fog can arrive very quickly – and he should never fail to establish a fix whenever possible. In addition, he should plan passages with great care making himself aware of all dangers likely to be encountered. Furthermore, he should ensure that he has the information needed to make any port within the cruising area – and near him as it does happen that weather conditions can dictate a change of plan. I would like to close this long, but not (I hope) boring, chapter with a further quote from *Reed's Almanac*: 'The successful navigator is he who takes nothing for granted, checks everything and prepares in advance, as far as possible, his books, charts and instruments, ready for all eventualities.'

5
The Navigator's Tools and Equipment

This chapter covers the various items the navigator needs on board to enable him to carry out his craft. They fall into three groups: information, measuring instruments and record-keeping logs (a fourth group, chart-table equipment, was dealt with in Chapter 4). In addition there are a number of electronic aids now on the market. These are not essential but are considered in Chapter 10.

Information

Under this heading come charts, maps, tidal atlases, almanacs, pilots and other booklets giving information about cruising areas and ports.

Charts

Rightly heading the list are the charts. These are now rather expensive but it is extreme folly to go to sea without a set of charts covering not only the planned cruising area but also adjoining areas which may be entered if plans are changed or the weather makes such a move a safer proposition.

As with all maps, the problem facing the cartographer is that he has to represent the curved surface of the earth on a flat piece of paper. Since it is impossible to achieve this without distorting something, charts are drawn to a number of systems – each chosen to fulfil particular requirements. Most common for cruising is Mercator's projection. This is drawn so that any straight line across the chart represents a line of constant bearing. Thus if a navigator takes a bearing of an object and draws a line on a Mercator's projection chart to represent that bearing, he knows that his ship lies on the line. Likewise, he can draw a line across the chart and measure the bearing to determine a course. However, there is a price to pay for this facility. The theory of chart projection is outside the scope of this book so sufficient to say that the main price is that the vertical distances on the chart are distorted, the lines of latitude gradually opening out as one moves either north or south of the equator. Since these lines of latitude would be an infinite distance apart at the poles, Mercator projection charts cannot be drawn to represent the polar areas. That is not likely to bother many readers. The second price is that the areas of land masses (and of sea areas) are badly distorted. If you look at a Mercator's chart of the world, Iceland and Borneo appear to be the same size whereas Borneo is over seven times the size of Iceland. However, these charts are drawn for navigators and navigators are not interested in areas.

Apart from direction, navigators are concerned with distance and so the chart distortion must be taken into consideration when measuring all distances on the chart. Fortunately a nautical mile is the distance between two lines of latitude one minute apart measured along a meridian (or line of longitude). Since minutes of latitude are marked on the vertical sides of every chart, these can be used as distance scales. It is important on small-scale charts to measure distances on that part of the margin which lies to one side or other of the part of the chart in use as the scale varies from top to bottom of such a chart (this is easily checked using a pair of dividers). On large-scale charts, as often used on small boats, this is not so important as the differences are very small. Nevertheless, it is good practice to follow the rule at all times as this avoids the risk of forgetting when it does matter. Of academic interest on short passages is the fact that on these charts a straight line does not represent the shortest distance between two points. The differences are too small to matter until one is thinking about crossing oceans.

Very large-scale charts and port plans are usually prepared using a different projection called Gnomonic. Without going into details, on these charts the lines of longitude all radiate from the pole and are, therefore, not parallel and the lines of latitude are curved. However, these distortions are so small that they cannot be detected on a large-scale chart of a small area. Unlike the Mercator's charts, these show land features without distortion and represent areas accurately. These charts are usually equipped with a scale similar to that found on ordinary maps and distances should be taken from this scale.

The Admiralty, and the firms of Stanford and Imray produce charts of all or part of the UK coastal waters.

As one would expect, the Admiralty offers a complete range including many large-scale harbour plans. All Admiralty charts are very detailed and include tidal information and sketches of the shore-line as seen from the sea where appropriate. The only disadvantage of these charts is their size which means a large chart table is required for accurate and comfortable work on them. They are supplied folded once, making them 71cm × 51cm (28in × 20in). A complete list of Admiralty charts is given in Catalogue NP131, while Catalogue NP109 covers the UK coastal waters and north-west Europe. Both catalogues can be obtained from chart agents.

Stanford produce a set of coloured folded charts specially designed for the yachtsman. The colours used effectively indicate deep and shallow water as well as areas that dry at low tide. Although less detail is given than on the Admiralty charts, there are plans of the major harbours and, printed on the reverse, pilotage notes for the area covered. These notes cover details of facilities available as well as navigational information. Tidal information is given in the form of small tidal stream chartlets for each hour. These charts offer excellent value for money but the series only covers the English Channel and the southern part of the North Sea. It comprises three passage charts and eight drawn to a larger scale including one for the Channel Islands.

The other company producing yachtsmen's charts is Imray. Three series are published which, between them, offer passage charts for the entire UK coastline. The 'C' charts cover from the Firth of Clyde, down the Irish Sea, through the English Channel and up the east coast as far as Newcastle. There are two passage charts covering the English Channel, the remainder being larger-scale charts of varying scales which include harbour plans for the area as well as tidal information. This latter is given in two forms as there are small chartlets showing the major tidal streams as well as tables giving details at selected points similar to the system used on Admiralty charts. Unfolded, these charts measure 79cm × 113cm (31in × 44in). The smaller 'Y' charts are easier to use on chart tables with limited space but cover a smaller area – from Land's End to The Wash – with the charts west of Start Point dealing with the harbours and estuaries only. The gaps between these two series are made good by the 'BB' charts which were published with the fishing community in mind.

Full details of the charts published by these companies can be obtained by writing to them at the addresses shown on page 190.

Ordinary maps are of little value to the navigator although there are times when a map will help to identify a land-based object marked on a chart where it is usually shown standing in isolation. They are, however, helpful when it comes to planning shore expeditions which are often an important part of any cruise, especially if children are involved. The best are the Ordnance Survey maps but a set of these is very expensive. We make do with a copy of the AA/Reader's Digest *Book of the Road* which we find answers most of our questions.

Nautical Almanacs
Apart from charts, a nautical almanac is the most valuable source of information available to the navigator. The nautical almanac is defined in my rather old dictionary as 'an official register of the days

of the year giving in advance positions of stars and other data to mariners'. This definition remains sound although the almanacs printed today carry far more 'other data' than is suggested by the dictionary even though the astronomical tables are still included. Most important is the inclusion of daily tidal data for a wide number of standard ports which enables the navigator to calculate the depth of water at any point and any time when read in conjunction with the soundings shown on the chart.

There are two nautical almanacs available to those who cruise around the United Kingdom. The long-established *Reed's Nautical Almanac* is aimed at seamen in general although the latest issue includes many items of interest to the small-boat owner whilst *The Macmillan & Silk Cut Nautical Almanac* was published for the first time in 1980 with the yachtsman in mind. Although I have been using *Reed's* for many years and thus feel a certain loyalty to that excellent publication, the Macmillan almanac is probably the one I shall carry in future. I put it like that as they are both fine publications and I would suggest that both are considered very seriously before deciding which one should be purchased.

The almanac will give you details of the International Regulations for Preventing Collisions at Sea – the 'rule of the road'. These should be known to all who leave harbour but, as they are clearly stated in the almanacs and as such an almanac should be carried at all times, they are not repeated in this book. Also included will be a passage on coastal navigation together with a number of useful tables such as those giving 'Distances Off for Rising and Dipping Lights' as well as worked examples of the various techniques used such as those described in the last chapter.

There is a complete list of lights to be found around the coast as well as details of other navigational aids such as radio stations. Radio Direction Finding is becoming a very popular method of fixing the ship's position and we shall be looking at that in Chapter 10. Radio is featured again in the section dealing with signals as are flags, sound signals, the use of flares and other distress signals etc.

Weather forecasting is not forgotten and a section covering the various forecasts available to the mariner is included. This will also help the seaman to develop his own forecasting skills. Since weather can cause problems, emergency equipment and notes on bad-weather tactics are also given.

Add to the above notes on how to deal with customs, details of harbours with notes on navigational problems as well as facilities to be found and a comprehensive set of tidal stream chartlets and it becomes obvious that an almanac is both required reading and a very important part of the navigator's (and skipper's) armoury.

Tidal Atlases

Tidal atlases give details of tidal streams in far greater detail than can be given in almanacs or on charts. Whilst not vital, they are useful, and especially so in areas where tides play an important part. In addition they often carry tables or diagrams which enable exact heights of tides and exact rates between springs and neaps to be found without calculation. Tidal atlases are published by the Admiralty and, for a limited area (the English Channel) by Stanford as well as by a number of other concerns whose publications cover areas of special interest to themselves. Although not essential in this country as the information on the charts and in the almanacs is usually more than adequate, these atlases come into their own in other parts of the world where they are the sole source of this data.

Pilots

Pilots or Sailing Directions are concerned with giving information about an area to assist the navigator in planning a safe passage and in executing that plan. Unlike almanacs, they are not reprinted annually as much of the information stays the same. Like charts, however, they should be kept as up-to-date as possible by noting in them any changes appearing in *Notices to Mariners*. These notices do not cover all types of data found in pilots, and the publishers may well print leaflets from time to time showing changes which should be noted. Publishers nearly always welcome additional information or corrections and it is a nice gesture to inform them if any omissions or errors are discovered. The same comment applies to almanacs.

The only pilot printed which covers the entire UK coastline is the *Cruising Association Handbook* – a veritable feast of information which also takes in some of continental Europe. Naturally a book which covers such a large area cannot offer great detail and there are a large number of pilots dealing with smaller areas. It is, however, ideal for those who wish to cruise over large areas including those who trail and sail. The *Handbook* divides the coastline into a number of short sections with passage notes for the area followed by details of the harbours which include instructions on the approach (with details of when such an approach is unsafe), notes on places where berths and anchorages may be found and what facilities are available. A good book to aid planning during the long winter evenings; my one criticism is that the abbreviations used can sometimes confuse.

Measuring Instruments

The Steering Compass

The principal measuring instrument carried on board is, of course, the ship's steering compass (see Plate 5.1). Since this will be required

Plate 5.1 A standard compass. Mounted in gimbals it must be viewed from above to avoid errors due to parallax (*Simpson Lawrence*)

almost constantly while at sea a great deal of thought should be given to the type best suited to the boat and to siting it in the best possible position. Since compass deviation can be made considerably worse by siting the compass near any large mass of metal, the choice of position can be limited. However, compensating magnets can be fitted to reduce the error as much as possible (really a job for the professional compass corrector) and, in any event, the compass will have to be swung (see pages 68–70). A known error is always acceptable; more important is the unknown error. This can be created by quite small metallic objects which can reasonably be in more than one place. An example is a gear lever which, if very close to the compass, can cause very different readings when in neutral as opposed to forward. Some parts of wheel-steering mechanisms can have a similar effect. Fortunately compasses come in a variety of sizes and shapes and it is usually possible to find one that can be placed in a suitable position whilst remaining easy to see from the helm regardless of which side the helmsman is sitting.

However, before looking at the types of enclosure available it is worth looking at the compass card itself. There was a time when all compasses showed only the traditional 32 points of the mariner's compass. Gradually it was realised that this system left much to be desired as each point is an inconvenient 11¼°. The result was that cards were marked with a numerical notation as well as the points. Two numerical notations were used – the Circular Notation with north being 0° (and 360°) and the card marked from 0 to 360 in a clockwise direction and the Quadrantal Notation which is more complicated (see Fig 5.1). On this card both north and south are marked 0°, east and west are marked 90° and the card marked from

0 to 90 in each quadrant. This means that north east becomes N45E (045 using the Circular Notation) and south west becomes S45W (or 225 using the Circular Notation). As can be seen, the Quadrantal Notation can be confusing and it is quite easy to make stupid mistakes when it is employed. Fortunately the system has almost entirely disappeared but there are still a few compasses fitted with this sort of card and they are offered at bargain prices. Even so, it is very sensible to give them as wide a berth as possible.

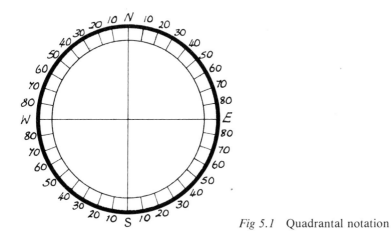

Fig 5.1 Quadrantal notation

In fact, as will be appreciated after reading the previous chapter, the Circular Notation is all that is required – and all that is found on most modern compasses. Apart from the traditional appearance of a compass which is marked in points as well as the Circular Notation, these extra markings have no advantage. Generally speaking a compass marked in increments of 5° is perfectly satisfactory as it is usually impossible to steer more accurately than that and a compass kept as simple as possible reduces the risk of error.

Now for enclosures. The traditional type of compass unit consists of a flat card suspended in a bowl containing damping oil to stop the card swinging too wildly. Such a compass is fitted with external gimbals and must be viewed from above. It must, therefore, be fitted below the helmsman's eye level and there can be problems with parallax when viewed from the sides of the cockpit. Such a unit is, therefore, more likely to be employed on larger craft fitted with wheel steering. The compasses can be supplied in a binnacle which is fitted with lights.

Because of the problems in siting these compasses, a new breed has come onto the market which are best described as dome compasses. The card is a segment of a hollow sphere – the sort of thing you get if you take a slice out of a tennis ball by cutting through 12mm (½in) or so either side of its 'equator' – fitted to a dished hub and mounted inside a clear spherical housing. Because of the shape and the oil filling, such a card will appear to be bigger than it is and so smaller units can be employed. Most dome-type compasses are fitted with internal gimbals and light sources so are much neater when installed – a point to remember if there is any risk of an errant headsail sheet tangling with the compass. These dome compasses are available with a variety of mounting units: bracket mounting, well mounting, bulkhead mounting and binnacle mounting.

Bracket mountings (see Plate 5.2) are the simplest to install being positioned on the cabin bulkhead or some other vertical, or near vertical, surface. An added advantage is that the compass can be taken from the mounting very easily and can be stored safely below when the boat is unattended.

The well mounting is let into a horizontal surface and can be a very neat arrangement (see Plate 5.3). Care must be taken to position it so as to avoid folk tramping on it and some find it inconvenient to have a compass low down in the cockpit rather than at the more usual eye level. This is, I believe, more a matter of taste than anything else.

Bulkhead mountings (sometimes called porthole compasses) should, in my view, be more popular than they are. The compass is mounted in a hole cut through the bulkhead and can be seen by both the helmsman and by those below albeit the reading from the cabin is

Plate 5.2 (*left*)   A bracket-mounted dome compass. It can be viewed from various angles without the reading becoming distorted. Note the magnification of the card which means a smaller card can be employed. This type can be lifted from the bracket and stowed away below for security when the craft is left unattended (*Simpson Lawrence*); *Plate 5.3* (*right*)   A well-mounted dome compass. It is internally gimballed and so can be dropped into a well cut in any suitable horizontal surface. Care has to be taken to site it where it will be protected from damage (*Simpson Lawrence*)

the reciprocal (ie 180° away from) of the course being steered. If any form of self-steering is fitted or if the boat is capable of sailing herself for short periods, it is comforting to be able to glance at the compass when below grabbing a cup of coffee or checking a chart. An incidental advantage of such compasses is that the design enables the manufacturer to include an inclinometer, which measures the angle of heel – into the compass. Not an essential instrument, it is an added bonus (see Plate 5.4).

Plate 5.4 A porthole compass. It is sited so that it can be read from both the cockpit and the cabin; it is rather less popular than it should be (*Simpson Lawrence*)

Plate 5.5 A binnacle-mounted dome compass. Owners of larger craft and those employing wheel steering often opt for this type (*Simpson Lawrence*)

Domed compasses in binnacles (see Plate 5.5) are generally associated with the modern type of wheel-steering pedestal but could, nevertheless, be fitted in other locations. Because of the limited field of view, it is unlikely that they would find their way onto craft steered by tiller. Because the spherical card is near the spherical bowl which carries the lubber line, errors owing to parallax are reduced. In any event, a number of these compasses are fitted with three lubber lines, the additional ones being at 45° either side of the true line. By adding or subtracting 45 to the given course, the helmsman can sit well to one side of the compass and use one of these other lines. This feature can greatly simplify the problem of finding a suitable position for the compass.

Plate 5.6 A grid compass. This type makes steering far easier and helps to avoid helmsman error; they are, however, more difficult to site than the dome type of compass (*Simpson Lawrence*)

There is one other type of compass that is rightly popular and which was developed for aircraft use – the grid compass (see Plate 5.6). Based on the traditional type of enclosure, its advantages may outweigh the problems of finding a good site. The glass covering the compass is able to rotate and carries two parallel lines about 13mm (½in) apart. Running round the outside of the casing is a fixed Circular Notation. The course required is set by rotating the glass cover until an arrow points at the required bearing on the casing. The card carries a heavy line linking north and south and the helmsman has only to keep this heavy line between and parallel to the lines etched on the glass cover to remain on course. The advantages of using a grid compass are that it is far less tiring to steer by one and the risk of a tired helmsman steering on the wrong course is eliminated. The disadvantages are that it is possible to steer on a reciprocal course by mistake – a rare but disastrous error – and the helmsman is less likely to be able to estimate the actual course steered if he is unable to hold the course ordered as can happen when sailing close to the wind or taking action to avoid another vessel.

The compass is one of the most important items on board and great care should be taken to select the right one for the job; nor should funds be skimped in this department. When making a choice remember that it is important that the compass be well lit. Various types of lighting are now available but if the usual filament lamps are employed these must be either red or green to avoid impairing night vision. It is worth paying extra to have a dimmer fitted and many modern compasses have this fitted as a standard feature or a standard extra.

The Hand-bearing Compass
We have already seen in Chapter 4 how the pelorus can be used for taking bearings, and a description of a home-made pelorus is shown in Fig 5.2. The more usual method is to use a hand-bearing compass although I prefer using the pelorus for a number of reasons. The most important is that the hand-bearing compass will suffer from error in exactly the same way as the steering compass and, whilst variation can be taken into account, there is no method of determining the deviation. Furthermore, I have found that hand-bearing compasses are very accident prone and can be difficult to read.

There are a number of types of hand-bearing compass on the market. The features to look for are a well-damped card and clear notation which is easy to read. Some models appear to project the numbers to infinity which avoids having to focus first on the object and then on the numbers which are very close. Some people, especially those with long sight, find compasses with this feature a great benefit.

Having suggested that there is little reason for carrying a hand-bearing compass, there is a strong case for carrying a compass that can be used as a boat compass and this can then double as a hand-bearing compass (see Plate 5.7). It is good practice to carry a boat compass – twice I have been caught in unexpected fog in an estuary that I know extremely well and, on both occasions, I was completely lost. Although there are clues to be noted, such as the direction of the stream, it is amazing how disorientated one can become in such conditions. On one of these trips I was forced to give up and return to the slip using the traffic noises and, later, shore lights, as a guide.

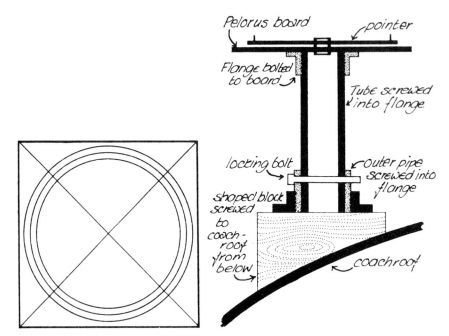

(a) The board marked up ready to have the compass rose glued in place. Although the board can be circular it is easier to align with the yacht's centreline if it is square. A straight edge can be placed along one side to simplify this if it is accurately made

(b) One method of fitting the pelorus. Note that this raises the board about 7in above the coachroof, making it look clumsy but enabling the observer to use the pelorus more easily. Remember that the pelorus will be used to take bearings aft of the beam when the observer will have to lie on the coachroof. On larger boats a higher and more robust mounting is advisable

Fig 5.2 Making a pelorus: Take a piece of plywood and cut it accurately to a 10in square. Find the centre by drawing onto it the two diagonals; see (a). Draw three circles at 4¼in radius, 4½in radius and 4¾in radius – pencil will do. Take a compass rose cut out of an old chart and firmly glue it to the plywood so that the two centres are exactly together (use a pin tapped into the ply for this) and so that the diagonals are lined up with the 45° and 135° marks on the outer, true, scale of the rose. Now use a ruler to extend the main divisions of the rose to the circles on the plywood. Take the 0°, 10°, 20° and so on to the outer circle and the 5°, 15°, 25° and so on to the middle circle. Again, a pencil will do and a fairly hard one, 2H or harder, should be used, so as to make a slight score into the ply as the line is drawn.

Next drill a hole through the exact centre about the size of a 2BA bolt and screw through it from the bottom a 2BA ¾in bolt putting a washer underneath. Top this with another washer and a nut and tighten it down. This bolt must be positioned as accurately as possible on the dead centre of the compass rose.

Now to make a pointer with sights. A strip of hardwood 8½in by ¾in and about ⅛in thick will do nicely. Draw a line along its length on the exact centreline on one side and then shape one end to a point, exactly on the line. Drill a hole on the line and half way along so that it will rotate easily on the 2BA bolt but not so large that it slops about. Drill two more very small holes, again on the line, about ½in from each end and drive two brass brads or panel pins through these holes from the bottom. File off the points.

Back to the board. This will have to be fixed in some position on the boat to give as clear a view all round as possible and so that the lubber line (0°–180°) is on, or parallel to, the centreline of the boat. It is a great help if it can be dismounted easily. One way which works well but requires a bit of trouble making is to bolt (don't use screws, they will soon work loose) a threaded pipe flange to the underside of the pelorus. Screw a 6in length of pipe into the flange as tightly as possible. By choosing the right size you will find that that pipe fits nicely into the next size up. Make two assemblies using a couple of inches of the bigger pipe screwed tightly into threaded flanges and fix these either on the coachroof or either side of the centreline wherever you decide to put them so that the flanges are horizontal (use packing). The pelorus will now stand in these (two because it is often very difficult to find one place with clear vision all round) and the only problem is to align it correctly. Position the pelorus in one of the holders and then drill a horizontal hole through both pipes just above the flange holding the larger pipe. Move the pelorus to the other fitting and position it. Drill another hole about ½in above the flange so that the two holes do not run into each other. It helps if the holes are displaced in the other direction, about 90° to each other. A bolt through the holes will keep the pelorus in position.

The last job is to give everything two good coats of varnish and then to fix the pointer onto the pivot using a washer both sides and two nuts above locked together (or one with a nylon insert)

Plate 5.7 A typical hand-bearing compass. It can be unclipped from the handle and fitted to a back-plate fixed in the tender to become a boat compass (*Simpson Lawrence*)

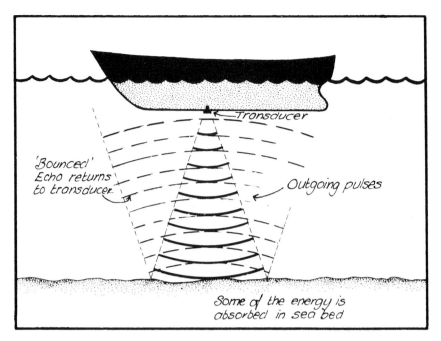

Fig 5.3 How an echo sounder works

Luckily there was a handy pub and the fog had lifted and dispersed by closing time so, as they say, all's well that ends well. Even so, I learned a valuable lesson.

Echo Sounders and Lead-lines
From looking around us, we must now turn our attention to what is below the keel and look at the various instruments available for measuring the depth of water and indicating the nature of the sea bed. To some extent we have covered this in Chapter 1.

Echo sounders all work on the same principle (see Fig 5.3). A pulse of electricity is passed from the read-out unit to a probe fixed to the hull called a transducer. This converts the electrical pulse into a minute ultrasonic pressure wave which passes out into the water over an angle to create a conical search area. When the pressure wave hits

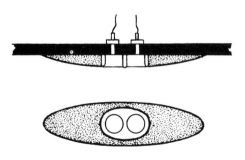

Fig 5.4 Fairing block around transducer(s) to smooth water flow

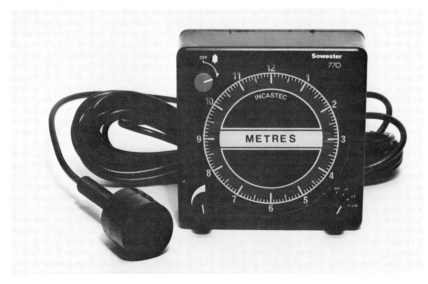

Plate 5.8 A rotating-arm type of echo sounder, offering three ranges (0–12 metres, 0–24 metres and 0–120 metres) and an alarm which may be set to sound between 1½ and 11 metres (*South Western Marine Factors*)

the sea bed some of this pressure wave is absorbed and some is reflected – to bounce back to the transducer or, in more expensive equipment, to a separate receiving transducer. Here the pressure wave is converted back into electricity which is amplified to give a signal on the read-out unit. This unit has to be able to measure the time it has taken for the pressure wave to travel to the sea bed and back again but, as the depth is proportional to this time, will show the result in units of depth.

There are a variety of types available on the market but, happily, the one most likely to be chosen is also the least expensive. This consists of a read-out unit which houses a rotating arm running around inside a scale (see Plate 5.8). The rotation of the arm provides the time base and all that happens is that a light set on its outer end flashes whenever the unit detects an electrical pulse. Thus, the out-going pulse shows as a flash against the zero mark and the incoming flash (or flashes) show against the appropriate depth. The engineering required is very basic and gives little trouble. However, older types used a neon flash and these tended to be unreliable. Modern units using gallium arsenide phosphide diodes do not suffer in the same way and this feature should be looked for when buying such an echo sounder.

There are two other problems. Some units have the centre of the dial raised which means that the viewing window is angled. Unless these are viewed from directly ahead the reading will be false owing to parallax. This can be solved by avoiding such models. The second problem is that in bright light the flashes can be quite difficult to see. There is no simple solution to this as fitting a viewing hood also restricts the angle of view and can make the instrument useless unless there is a spare person available to operate it.

Only one operator adjustment is required. As a certain amount of the pressure wave is absorbed by the bottom and that amount varies – soft mud absorbing most and hard rock least – there must be control over the power of the pulse being transmitted. This is known as the gain control and the object is to adjust this until a single reading is obtained. This will be the most powerful reflection and will almost certainly be from the sea bed. Assuming that this is set for soft mud and the boat then moves over a rocky area, a number of additional echoes will be detected. These are caused by the powerful reflected pressure waves 'bouncing' between the transducer and the sea bed and will indicate the actual depth, twice the depth and, sometimes, even deeper indications. As the boat returns to the mud, the pressure wave, now reduced in power, will become more and more absorbed and the signal will fade away – more punch is required to obtain an echo.

Fish and other matter suspended in the water will also produce signals which cannot always be eliminated. However, it is rare that such signals can be confused with the echo from the sea bed.

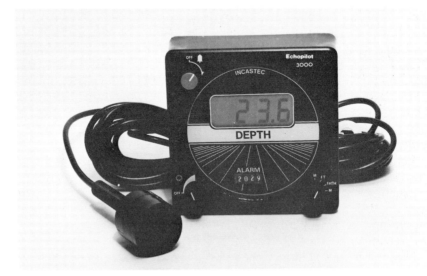

Plate 5.9 A digital-read-out type of echo sounder. When the instrument fails to detect a firm reading, the figure pulse-indicates the last good reading. This feature goes some way towards overcoming the problems mentioned in the text (*South Western Marine Factors*)

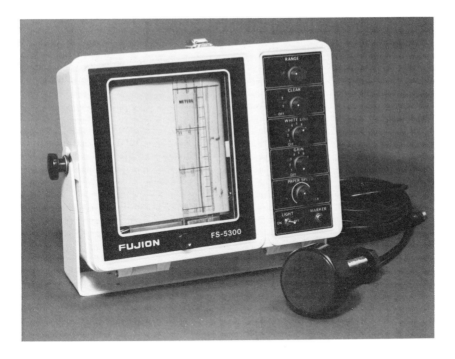

Plate 5.10 A paper-recording type of echo sounder (*South Western Marine Factors*)

There are other types of echo sounder available. A moving-coil meter type has been developed to overcome the difficulty of reading the flasher unit in bright light. Unfortunately there are other problems with these units and they are best avoided. Digital units (see Plate 5.9) are based on the same principles as the moving-coil meter type and share the problems as well as being difficult to read. Cathode-ray-tube units and paper-trace types (the latter is shown in Plate 5.10) are excellent but must be housed below as they are not waterproof. Designed for the world of commerce, they are expensive and not really suited to small boats.

Echo sounders of the rotating-arm type are generally reliable if they are properly installed. Manufacturers supply full installation instructions and these should be followed slavishly. Generally speaking it is a mistake to try to avoid yet another hole in the hull by mounting the transducer(s) inside the hole. Such installations are far less sensitive.

No matter how much faith is placed in the echo sounder there is always the risk that such faith will prove to have been misplaced and it will be to the good, old-fashioned lead that the skipper turns for help (see Fig 5.5). As has been mentioned, the lead-line is best marked in a style that does not rely on memory as any arbitrary system is easily forgotten unless used very frequently. Since charts

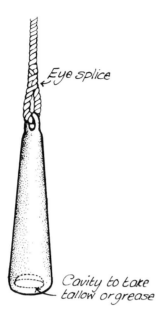

Eye splice

Cavity to take
tallow or grease

Fig 5.5   The hand lead

now show depths in metres, a number of different methods have been
suggested which use the old traditional types of marks (which can be
read by feel when it is dark) placed at metric intervals. However, it is
rare indeed that a torch is not available and a logical system that can
be easily remembered is, in my view, preferable. The argument that a
torch should not be used as it destroys night vision is negated if the
same torch has to be used to check a mark against a table or list. I
have found the method described in Chapter 1 to be as good as any.

Even so, it takes a certain amount of practice to be able to use a
lead without getting soaked to the skin and ending up with a horrible
tangle of line around one's feet. It pays to use it fairly often rather
than to forget its existence until it is desperately needed. Stowing the
lead-line can be difficult as the heavy lead makes hanging it by the coil
of line impractical; ours is kept in a small canvas bag hanging in the
cockpit.

Now, neither echo sounder nor lead will give you the figure you
actually want. This will be either the depth of water or the depth
under the keel. Since the echo sounder measures the depth from the
transducer and the lead the depth from the leadsman's hand, the
following four constants should be known:

Depth from transducer to keel
Depth from water surface to transducer
Depth from hand to keel
Depth from hand to water surface

These should be noted in a handy spot so that they can be applied to
the reading obtained to give the figure required.

Logs

The last measuring instrument of importance is the log. Once these measured only distance run and some modern types still offer the same figure. Others give speed whilst some now offer both speed and distance run. Since the navigator is interested in plotting distance run there is merit in an instrument which gives this figure although it can be calculated if the speed is known – assuming that the speed is fairly constant and that any changes have been noted in the deck log.

There are four types available on the market of interest. The oldest consists of a rotor streamed at the end of a special line attached to the instrument, the instrument itself slotting onto a special fitting on the stern or on one quarter (see Plate 5.11). As the rotor turns, so does the line which, in turn, drives a gear train inside the instrument and thus the pointers which indicate the distance run. There is a danger that the rotor will pick up weed or some other matter (old plastic bags being a fairly frequent catch in these pre-packaged days) resulting in a false reading. However, it is a fairly simple matter to haul the line aboard and clear away such rubbish. There is also the risk that the line will snag and break and a spare line and rotor should be carried at all times. The line has to be hauled aboard before stopping as it will otherwise hang down below and almost certainly catch on the bottom.

Plate 5.11   The famous Walker log: a superb example of a mechanical type of log of the traditional type (sometimes called a taffrail log)

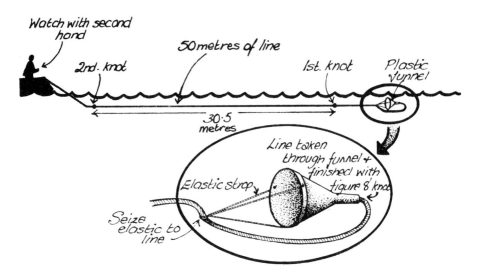

Fig 5.6 An emergency log that can be streamed to determine speed. Method: cast log, start timing when first knot passes through fingers and stop as second knot passes. To haul in, just pull. Elastic stretches and funnel capsizes

Seconds	120	60	30	20	15	12	10
Speed (knots)	0.5	1.0	2.0	3.0	4.0	5.0	6.0

To avoid the risk of lost lines and the need to stream and haul as required, logs were designed with tiny rotors protruding through small holes in the hull (see Plate 5.12). Every rotation of the rotor or paddle wheel causes an electrical impulse to be passed to the instrument which could show distance run or, by comparing the pulse rate with a time base, speed. It is true that fouling is less frequent but, when it happens, it is far harder to cure. These units are designed to be removed from inside the hull but this is not always possible and almost always extremely difficult. Although the hole left is very small, the amount of water it can take during the operation is frightening. This is not, however, the main drawback. Since these units are left in place all the time, there is almost bound to be a gradual build up of weed and other marine growth on the rotor which will cause errors.

Logs are now available which combine features from the above. The rotor is streamed but, with these logs, the line is a static cable which brings the electrical pulses back to the instrument (see Plate 5.13). The risks of the rotor becoming tangled up with debris and the whole lot being lost remain and the same comments apply in that direction. Being electrically operated, the reading can be in either speed or distance run and some models offer both. It is a simple matter to position the instrument where required even if this creates difficulties in reading it as repeaters can be linked to it. With the mechanical type, which also requires careful positioning, this facility is not available and may create problems if the boat does not have an

Plate 5.12 A rotating log, in this case with digital read-out, operated by a paddle wheel installed through the hull (*South Western Marine Factors*)

Plate 5.13 A trailing electronic log. Each rotation of the rotor sends an impulse to the unit. The instrument compares the number of impulses to a time base to provide the speed and a distance-run counter is also incorporated (*Simpson Lawrence*)

aft cockpit, as this means that those who favour centre cockpits must send a crewmember aft to read the mechanical log which, in some weather conditions, may place them at risk. A further word may be in place regarding reading mechanical logs. This is one of the duties that can be given to younger members of the crew but it must be remembered that with the mechanical log the line itself is also rotating. Long hair blown by the wind can catch around it and be wound up, dragging the reader's head down to it. This is not only very painful but highly dangerous. Anyone with long hair should wear a hat of some sort when reading the log. This does not apply to the electrical log as the cable remains static and only the rotor turns.

The electro-magnetic log solves the problems caused by rotors by eliminating them. Two electrodes protrude from the hull and as water passes between them a small current is produced which varies with the speed of the water flow. This log, therefore, measures speed although some models calculate distance run using a form of inbuilt calculating machine. They are less accurate than the rotor types, especially at low speeds and also suffer from marine growth being permanent installations.

The Doppler type operates on a similar principle to the echo sounder in that it sends out a pressure wave and notes its return. However, instead of measuring the time taken it measures any change in frequency which, thanks to the Doppler effect, can be used to calculate speed. In shallow water the echo will bounce from the sea bed and give speed over the ground instead of speed through the water. This makes it sound very attractive, but it is not as simple as that. At some depth (what depth depending on the state of the water) the echo will fail to reach the bottom but will be returned by suspended matter floating in the water. It will then cease to give speed over the ground and join its cousins in giving speed through the water. The main problem is that it is impossible to know which is being offered except in very shallow and very deep water.

Although other types of log can be bought, they are not suited to the fairly slow speeds of the average cruising boat. The traditional mechanical type has proved itself to be both reliable and accurate and is generally the first choice for boats with an aft cockpit so that the log can be read from its safety. For the reasons already stated, consideration should be given to the combined type if such an installation cannot be achieved in which case a repeater should be fitted in the cockpit or over the chart table. Marine growth, vegetable and animal, on the fixed rotor types causes so much trouble that this type is best ignored.

Inclinometer (or Clinometer)

Before leaving measuring instruments, mention should be made of the inclinometer. By no means essential, these are cheap and simple devices consisting of a weighted pendulum swinging in front of a scale marked in degrees which indicates the angle of heel.

Keeping Records – The Logs

We have seen that the art of coastal navigation consists of maintaining as accurate a plot of the ship's track as possible and checking it as often as possible by any means available. No navigator can maintain the plot unless the information required is available. It should be a golden rule that all watchkeepers note every change in speed or direction, no matter how small, as well as details of any sightings (with bearings if possible) which may assist the navigator. It is helpful if changes in weather conditions are also noted.

Human nature being what it is, this rule is more likely to be followed if the job is kept as simple and straightforward as possible and a ruled deck log works far better than a simple notebook or, even worse, scraps of paper. Such a log can include columns for the navigator to complete so as to remove the risk of the helmsman mishearing or forgetting a verbal order.

Under the remarks column should be noted the name and brief description of any vessel close enough to identify. This takes very little trouble and it is just possible that the vessel will go missing in which case the sighting report could be of considerable assistance to HM Coastguard in the event of a search and rescue operation being mounted. This applies whether or not a radio is carried. Naturally, those with radio may hear about the problem earlier than those without but there are times when old information is better than none at all.

In addition to the deck log, there should be an official ship's log in which matters of all kinds to do with the boat and its journeys should be noted. This can include details of maintenance and repairs as such information can be of assistance when selling the craft.

Some people also keep their own personal logs but how far this is taken is a matter of personal choice. Few probably take it as far as we do but then we use these old logs as a source of copy when we are writing. A number of folk have told me that they wish they had taken more trouble. Memories fade and an old log book enables one to relive a cruise from the comfort of an armchair during the depths of winter – as good a way of spending a wet and miserable weekend as any!

6

The Signposts of the Sea

There was a time when the only signposts available to the mariner were the natural features of the coastline. Gradually, as the centuries have passed, all manner of navigational aids have been installed from great, storm-lashed lighthouses standing as monuments to their builders to simple poles pushed into the mud at the side of a creek to mark the channel. Naturally, we must learn to recognise these signposts and be able to identify them on our charts. We must also learn the various descriptions and abbreviations to be found in the almanacs and pilots as well as on the charts so that we can know what to look out for.

One danger is that we shall incorrectly identify some navigational aid and no navigator worth his salt will be satisfied until every navigational aid seen has been positively identified. There is an old saying which remains very true – 'a buoy in the right place at the right time is not always the right buoy'. The same applies to every signpost of the sea be it natural, such as a headland, or man made.

Lights

Many different types of signposts are lit these days and so it is sensible to start with the various types of light employed and to learn the names and abbreviations used to describe them. Table 6.1 shows these in graphic form. The following comments may help to establish the vital points:

The period is the time from the start of one sequence to the start of the next. It is stated in seconds (eg 5s) in descriptions.

Occulting lights are those where the total duration of light exceeds the total duration of darkness whilst *flashing lights* are those where the total duration of the light is less than that of the darkness. Because the eye can detect extremely quick flashes but not quick occulting, flashing lights are subdivided as shown. The actual rates are:

Quick Flashing 50 to 79 flashes per minute (usually 50 or 60)

Very Quick Flashing 80 to 159 flashes per minute (usually 100 or 120)

Ultra Quick Flashing 160+ flashes per minute (usually 240 or 300)

Table 6.1 Light Characteristics

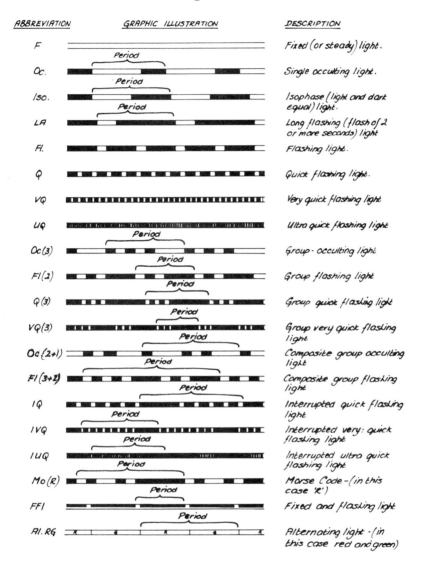

ABBREVIATION	GRAPHIC ILLUSTRATION	DESCRIPTION
F		Fixed (or steady) light.
Oc.		Single occulting light.
Iso.		Isophase (light and dark equal) light.
LFl		Long flashing (flash of 2 or more seconds) light
Fl.		Flashing light.
Q		Quick flashing light.
VQ		Very quick flashing light
UQ		Ultra quick flashing light
Oc(3)		Group-occulting light
Fl(2)		Group flashing light
Q(3)		Group quick flashing light
VQ(3)		Group very quick flashing light
Oc(2+1)		Composite group occulting light
Fl(3+2)		Composite group flashing light
IQ		Interrupted quick flashing light
IVQ		Interrupted very: quick flashing light
IUQ		Interrupted ultra quick flashing light
Mo(R)		Morse Code - (in this case 'R')
FFl		Fixed and flashing light
Al. RG		Alternating light - (in this case red and green)

Any letter may be used for lights flashing the Morse code; it happens that the one shown in the table is the letter R. Naturally, letters where the code used is either composed entirely of dots or entirely of dashes are not so described as they are indistinguishable from normal group flashing lights.

Seven colours are used; the abbreviations are shown in the almanac. If the colour of a light is not specified, it may be taken as being white.

′ There has been a good deal of confusion regarding the range of a
light. The figure quoted on modern charts is the so-called 'luminous
range' – the distance at which the light could be seen regardless of the
curvature of the earth. Since it can well be over the horizon at that
range, especially when viewed from the cockpit of a small boat, this
is not the distance at which one would expect to see the light.
Reference must be made to the tables for Rising and Dipping Lights
referred to in Chapter 4. Only when the range is *less* than the
distance given for a light of a particular elevation is it important.
Range is quoted in miles. From this it follows that the elevation of a
light is of considerable importance. This is usually quoted in metres
(m) but may be in feet (f).

Let us now look at a few typical light specifications and try to see
what we should be looking for. First, the extract from the almanac
'Start Point – 50 13.3N/3 38.5W Fl(3) 10s 62m 25M. W round Tr vis
184°–068°; RC; FR 55m 12M (same Tr) vis 210°–255° over Skerries
Bank. Siren 60s'. The chart would omit the references to arcs of
visibility as these would be drawn on the chart using pecked lines
carrying the appropriate details. Now, to untangle the code. The light
is positioned as indicated at 50°13′ 3″ north and 3°38′ 5″ west. It is a
group flashing light with three flashes every 10sec. The light is 62m
above MHWS (see next chapter for definition of Mean High Water
Springs) and has a range of 25 miles, well in excess of our distance
from it when it is on the horizon – the tables for dipping and rising
lights quote the distance as about 20 miles for an observer 4m above
sea level. The light is white round the tower (the colour is only
specified because of the additional light) which is visible over the arc
indicated. These bearings are from the boat to the light – not from
the light to the boat. In this case, the limitation is caused by terrestrial
features and has no significance. The tower carries a Circular
Radiobeacon (RC) used for Radio Direction Finding. There is a fixed
red light with an elevation of 55m and a range of 12 miles carried on
the same tower with an arc of visibility as shown over the Skerries
Bank. The distance off when observed from the cockpit would be
about 18 miles so this range is important. In this case, the arc of
visibility is deliberate as the light shines over an area of shallow water
called the Skerries – as a warning of that specific danger. Lastly, the
fog signal is a siren which is sounded every 60sec.

As you enter the harbour at Lymington in Hampshire, the channel
is marked by six lights. At the entrance is a buoy (which enjoys the
name of 'Jack in the Basket') which is specified as Fl R2s – a flashing
red light, one flash every 2sec. This buoy we shall leave to port as we
enter. The opposite side of the channel is marked by a buoy Fl G2s –
a similar light which flashes green instead of red and which we leave
to starboard.

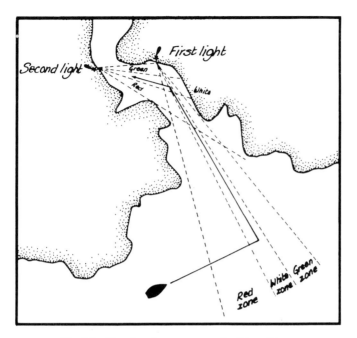

Fig 6.1 Sketch of entrance to the River Dart

As we approach the harbour proper there is another buoy to be left to port marked QR – a quick flashing red light. Mounted on the hill and affixed to the two beacons which line up with the entrance to the channel are two more lights, FR or fixed red, whilst the rail-ferry terminal on the opposite side of the river is marked by 2FG(vert) – 2 fixed green lights vertically mounted.

Already we can see a pattern emerging. In simple terms, if the light is a red one, leave it to port as you enter; if it is a green one, leave it to starboard. Naturally, the reverse is true when leaving harbour.

Generally speaking – there are some exceptions – fixed lights are used to mark leading beacons. These are lined up for part of the time, as shown on the chart, to bring the boat in clear from danger. The chart or harbour plan must be consulted to determine what part of the channel is so marked; it is extremely dangerous to assume that leading lights indicate a straight run in.

Still speaking generally, marinas, ferry pontoons, landing slips and other similar obstructions within the harbour are lit with two vertical lights: red when to port and green when to starboard.

Let us go west and look at another series of lights in the river Dart in Devon. Facing the entrance is a light described thus: Iso WRG 3s 9m 8M vis G318°–325° W325°–331° R331°–340°. A bit further in is a seond light with a similar description – Fl WRG 2s 5m 6M vis G280°–289° W289°–297° R297°-shore. If you refer to the sketch plan of the harbour (see Fig 6.1) all will become clear. These lights are so arranged that one is safe so long as the white light is visible. Move too far to the port, and the red sector becomes visible – move too far to starboard and we see the green sector. We simply work in using the white sector of the first light until we see the white sector of the second light and then change course. For the record, the first light is an isophase light (duration of light equal to duration of dark) with a period of 3sec, thus showing light for 1½sec and darkness for 1½sec. The second light is a single flash every 2sec.

Note that the same colour rule applies, leave red to port and green to starboard.

So much for a simple channel. There are, of course, many areas where there is an obstruction in the channel which splits it into two. Here Cardinal Marks are used. We will look at the shape of these in the next section but the lights are as follows:

North   White VQ or Q (very quick or quick)
East   White VQ(3) every 5sec or Q(3) every 10sec
South   White VQ(6) + long flash every 10sec or Q(6) + long flash
        every 15sec
West   White VQ(9) every 10sec or Q(9) every 15sec

It is not important to remember the details. A continuously flashing light is north, a short burst is east, a medium burst and long flash is south and a long burst is west. Remember continuous, short, medium, long – and the rest will follow.

Cardinal marks are positioned to the indicated side of the obstruction – a north cardinal mark being to the north of the obstruction it

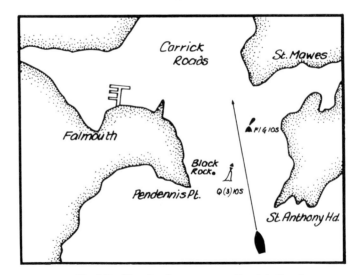

Fig 6.2   Sketch of entrance to Carrick Roads

marks – and often only that part nearest to a channel is marked. If, for example, a channel is running north-south and there is an area of shallows which splits the channel into two but the western channel is deeper and wider than the eastern one which is, therefore, rarely used, the middle ground will certainly be marked by a west cardinal mark and there may be either a north mark or a south mark (or both) if the main channel is tortuous and such marks would be helpful. A more typical example is the marking of an isolated danger such as the Black Rock in the entrance to the Carrick Roads off Pendennis Point near Falmouth. This rock is marked by an east cardinal mark which, as the entrance is running almost due north-south, means it is left to port. A flashing green light set slightly further in and to the east should be left to starboard. Thus the safe channel is clearly signposted (see Fig 6.2).

Buoys and Marks

To a large extent, the various buoys and perches (poles set in the mud at the side of channels) have obvious meanings if the above is understood.

Port-hand marks are coloured red. Buoys are can-shaped as are topmarks where fitted. Spars (the technical name for perches) may be fitted with can-shaped topmarks made from one of the new reflecting plastics which make them very easy to find using a torch or spotlight.

Starboard-hand marks are coloured green. Buoys are conical shaped and the topmarks are cones with the point pointing upward. Spars may be fitted with reflecting topmarks as described above.

Cardinal marks are always yellow and black and carry black topmarks. These are sketched in Fig 6.3 and, as can be seen, it is very easy to remember north, pointing up, and south, pointing down. East and west are harder to memorise but can be remembered as follows: working clockwise we work from 'up and up' through 'up and down' through 'down and down' to 'down and up'. Compare this with the sketches and you will see how it works.

Three special types of mark should be remembered as well as the above. Isolated dangers are sometimes marked by a buoy or perch painted black and red, the bands running horizontally. Lights, if fitted, are always white group flashing (2). Safe-water marks, which may be found in mid-channel or as a landfall mark, are painted red and white, the bands running vertically. Again lights, when fitted, are white but various rhythms are employed – usually isophase or occulting.

The third is not often found. It is a yellow buoy of any shape and the light, if fitted, is also yellow. These buoys have no navigational significance and are laid for a variety of other purposes. Ignore them.

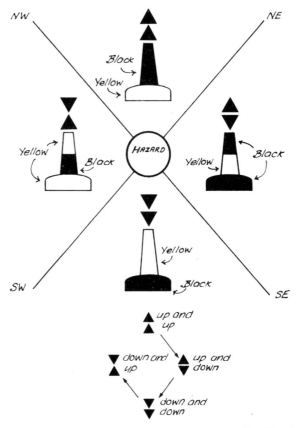

Fig 6.3 Cardinal marks

It may be noticed that there is no mention of wreck buoys. Since the above new buoyage system came into being, they have been dropped and such dangers are marked exactly as a natural hazard would be.

Leading Marks

Many channels are marked by objects ashore, often lit as described above, which are kept in line to ensure that the boat remains on the best course. Such a wide variety of marks is used that general comment is impossible. They are marked on the charts and often described in the almanacs and pilots. The vital thing is to ensure that the leading marks are properly identified before any reliance is placed upon them. A bearing is always quoted against such leading lines and should be used to check that the course is correct. Quite simply, if you think the leading marks are in line but the course you are steering does not agree with the bearing given, you have made a mistake and that top red light is marking some road works and not a navigational aid. It is extremely easy to make such errors.

Incidentally, one of the biggest problems when approaching almost every harbour is to differentiate between the shore lights that abound and the navigational lights. In some cases you will find comments in the pilot highlighting this problem – comments such as 'there is a bright white light over the entrance to a hotel which is often mistaken for . . .'.

Perches

Channels in smaller creeks are often marked by poles pushed into the mud. Time was when these were unpainted and advice had to be taken as to which side of the channel they had been placed. Usually one left them to port when working up to the head of the creek but there were a number of exceptions.

In busier places, these old-type perches have been replaced by either red or green poles often fitted with reflecting topmarks as

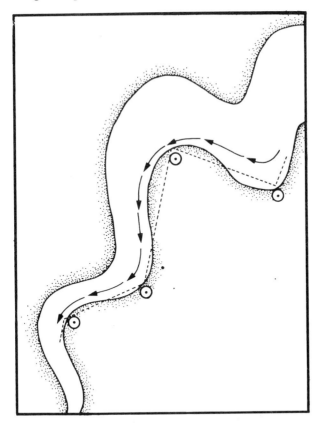

Fig 6.4 Marked channels. Steering on straight lines to just scrape past beacons may create problems: keep well clear and try to follow the sweep of the channel – it will be shown on the chart

already described. However, it should be borne in mind that channels do not make abrupt changes in direction and some compensation for this should be made. Fig 6.4 illustrates the point.

Traffic Signals

Whether traffic signals can be described as signposts is arguable. They are, however, there to be obeyed and serve exactly the same function as traffic lights do on our roads. The odd thing is that folk who would never dream of driving their car through a red light will happily ignore the marine equivalent when in their boat. There's none so queer as folk!

Traffic signals are normally confined to harbour entrances and the exact signals used are not standardised. The almanacs and pilots give full details and should be checked before entering any port which handles ferries, other commercial vessels or is used by the navy. These signals can be quite complicated and the easiest way to tackle the job is to work out, well in advance, those which give you the right of entry. Make a note of them somewhere handy – such as the deck log – and you then know that anything else means the same thing as a terrestrial red light, at least as far as you are concerned.

Let us look at Dover as an example. This harbour has two entrances and we decide to use the eastern of the two. The almanac tells us that by day 3 red balls in a triangle indicates no entry but departure is permitted, 2 red balls vertically hung indicates entry is allowed but not departure whilst 3 red balls vertically hung shows that the entrance is closed to traffic. Right, all we want to see are 2 red balls – nothing else need be remembered as everything else means 'no entry'. We do not even have to remember the various patterns used at this stage although we will when the time comes to leave. The night signals would be treated in the same way.

Pilotage using Signposts

It should be remembered when piloting in confined waters that the position of buoys as marked on the chart gives only the position of the mooring. As the buoys are free to swing, they can be quite a long way from the mooring – the lower the tide the further away they can be. Whilst the navigation authorities use the shortest possible scope to reduce the error as much as possible, some buoys in exposed sites must have a generous amount of ground tackle if they are not to drag – the problem is the same as it is for anchoring a boat. It follows that it is wise to use shore marks and other unmovable objects whenever possible when bearings are taken.

7
The Tides

Despite the fact that the weather can play such an obvious and important part in any cruise, the single natural force which has the greatest impact upon us is the tidal flow. The constant changes in the depth of water dictate when and if we can navigate in certain parts of our cruising ground whilst many harbour entrances are safe only during certain parts of the tidal cycle. The horizontal movements of the water – the tidal flows – can, as we have already seen, enable us to make journeys in times which would be impossible without their aid. The tide is, indeed, a fine friend and an implacable enemy. To make the best use of this free and natural force it is helpful if we have a thorough understanding of the subject.

Effect of Moon and Sun

Early mariners soon noticed that there was a connection between the moon and the tides, but it was not until Newton discovered the forces due to gravity that any explanation was found. He determined that all masses attract each other, the amount of that attraction being a function of the sizes of the masses and the distances between them. All the objects in the solar system are, therefore, subject to a complex and constantly changing combination of gravitational forces as the relative positions of the sun, planets and moons vary. It is by comparing the movements of the various bodies with the sizes of them and the distances between them that scientists calculate their weights and, indeed, are able to predict the presence of hitherto unknown planets before they are seen for the first time.

Fortunately, we are not concerned with all the complexities of the solar system but only with the forces which create a change in the gravitational pull on the earth's surface. The two bodies which have the greatest influence are our moon, being close to us, and the sun, being extremely large. Because the sun is distant, the effect that it has on the gravitational force is about a quarter of that exerted by the moon, so we will look at the moon first ignoring, for a moment, the sun's contribution.

As we would expect, the gravitational pull of the moon is greatest on that part of the earth's surface directly below it at any given moment and at its lowest on that part diametrically opposite. It has been calculated that the Great Pyramid weighs some 19 tons less when the moon is overhead than it does when the moon faces the opposite side of the earth.

Now, although the Great Pyramid may be feeling a lot lighter than usual from time to time there is little it can do about it as it stands firmly in the sand. Water, however, can move and so is constantly seeking the point of greatest gravitational attraction – a point which is also constantly on the move. A further complication which has yet to be explained satisfactorily (a personal view, there are a number of theories but I find none of them satisfactory) is that the water does not seek just the point of greatest attraction but a point which is diametrically opposite as well – the point of lowest attraction. Fig 7.1 shows the phenomenon as it would be if there were no land masses to take into consideration.

Fig 7.1   Water distorted by the moon's gravitational pull

As the earth rotates once every 24 hours and the moon orbits the earth once every 27½ days, give or take a few hours, the moon 'appears' to orbit around the earth every 24 hours 50 minutes during which time we would expect there to be two high tides and two low tides. In general, this is true – we will consider the exceptions later.

We will now look at the effect of the sun. Twice during each lunar cycle of 27½ days, the moon, sun and earth are in line. This occurs at the new and full moon. At these times (see Fig 7.2) the forces of the sun and moon combine, resulting in a greater range of tide (the difference between high water and low water) than average. Twice, the moon is to one side of the earth – at the time when the moon is in its quarters (see Fig 7.3) – when the force of the moon is reduced by that of the sun and the range is less than average.

The larger tides are known as 'springs' and the lower ones as

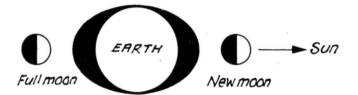

Fig 7.2   Spring tides caused by the combined pull of moon and sun

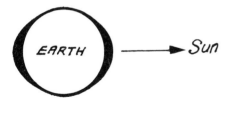

Moon in first quarter

EARTH ———▶ Sun

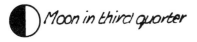

Moon in third quarter

Fig 7.3 Neap tides caused by sun's pull reducing moon's effect

'neaps'. The range gradually increases from neaps to springs over a period of about 7 days after which it decreases for the next 7 days so giving a fortnightly cycle.

To complicate the matter further, the forces vary from time to time. The greatest, resulting in the highest spring tides, are when the moon and sun both have low declination (ie are above the equator) – a state of affairs to be found at the equinoxes in March and September. Meanwhile, in addition, the moon's orbit is elliptical and, as one would expect, its gravitational attraction is less when it is further away and greater when the distance closes.

Fortunately for us, others bury their heads under wet towels and carry out the complicated calculations required to produce the tide tables which predict the time of high and low water and the height of both above a base line called the 'chart datum'.

Right, we can see a pattern of springs and neaps which will vary in range depending on the various forces exerted by the sun and the moon. But the earth is not just a globe covered with water, the water is constrained by the various land masses. Just as a river at its mouth may be in spate some days after the rains have fallen on the mountains in which it rises, so the effects of these forces are felt some time after they have been applied. The average delay is a couple of days so, for example, one would expect the highest springs of the month two days after the full and new moons.

The land masses complicate the entire issue so that there are some places in the world which experience only one tide per day whilst others, notably around the Solent, have four periods of high water instead of the usual two. Furthermore, areas of enclosed water such as the Mediterranean experience virtually no tidal effect as the water just does not move in and out through the Strait of Gibraltar quickly enough to change the water level.

Effect of Weather

The last complication to consider is the effect of the weather on the tides. Whereas we can ignore all that has gone before and just refer to the tide tables which will give us the answers we want whether we understand how they are arrived at or not, the effect of the weather cannot be tabulated and we must work it out for ourselves.

The barometric pressure has a marked effect on the tide even if it is small. Generally speaking, the only time that this matters is if we are fast aground (either accidentally or deliberately for laying up purposes) and we want to know whether or not we are likely to float off. The rule is simple: tidal predictions are calculated for average barometric pressure (1,000 millibars or 29½in) and there will be an increase in height of 0.3m (1ft) for every 34 millibars (1in) reduction in pressure and a similar decrease in height when the pressure is above average. The effect may not be immediate. Unusually intense local depressions can raise the sea level by as much as a metre in a surprisingly short period of time.

Prolonged heavy wind can also disturb the predictions, either by holding back (or bringing forward) the tide or by reducing the volume of the tidal flow. In the first case it can mean that high water, for example, can be as much as an hour earlier or later than expected and, in the second case, that the final height may be considerably affected. The stronger the wind and the longer it blows, the more marked the effect.

When a gale suddenly blows up, a 'storm surge' or wave may run along the coast which can, in exceptional circumstances, increase the height of the sea by as much as 2m; a negative storm surge will lower it by a similar amount.

Luckily for us, most of these exceptional disturbances occur only during very bad weather conditions when we are, if we are wise, either comfortably anchored in a harbour or, as Peter Heaton suggests in his excellent book *Sailing*, contemplating golf as an alternative sport (his suggestion to sailors when wind forces reach 12 on the Beaufort Scale). For the vast majority of the time we can ignore these 'meteorological effects' apart from noting that the next tide may be a bit later or a bit higher than we would otherwise expect.

Terms, Definitions and Calculations

We must now look at some of the terms used in relation to tides and how to calculate from them. The definitions of the various terms used below can be checked by referring to Fig 7.4.

Chart Datum is the starting point for all our depth calculations.

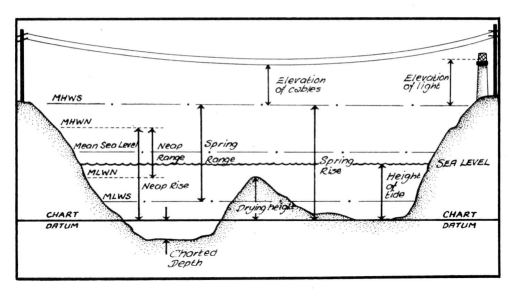

Fig 7.4 Terms used to describe tidal depths, etc

Recently charts and tide tables have been adjusted so that Chart Datum is at the level of the Lowest Astronomical Tide (LAT) which, as the name implies, is the lowest tide predictable taking into consideration the various factors we have already discussed but assuming average weather conditions. Thus all Charted Depths and Drying Heights are measured from Chart Datum, and the heights of the tides shown in tide tables also shown using Chart Datum as the base line.

It is, therefore, a simple matter to calculate the expected depth of any place at either high water or low water. We merely look up the predicted tide height in the tide tables and add it to the depth shown on the chart – or subtract from it the drying height.

Between HW and LW we have to carry out a further calculation. Step one is to work out the range of the appropriate tide which we do by subtracting the height at low water from the height at high water. This is the amount the height will increase during the time between those two tides, normally 6 hours. However, it does not rise at a uniform rate and a good, if approximate, method of calculation is the 'twelfths rule'. This states that the increase in the depth will be:

First hour	1 twelfth	Fourth hour	3 twelfths
Second hour	2 twelfths	Fifth hour	2 twelfths
Third hour	3 twelfths	Final hour	1 twelfth

Having determined the rise using this rule, we add back the height at LW and apply this to the charted depth or drying height as above. It is worth looking at an example, choosing a falling tide to reverse the calculation.

It is 1115 hours; high water was at 0915 when the height was 4.4m, low water will be at 1527 and the height predicted is 1.1m. We are approaching an area of shallow water where the charted depth is 0.3m and we draw 2.2m. Will we be able to pass over the shallow area?

Range $= 4.4 - 1.1 = 3.3$m
Time since HW is 2 hours. We shall, therefore, have lost 3 twelfths of the range $= 0.825$m
Height of tide at 1115 $= 4.4 - 0.83 = 3.57$m
Actual depth $= 3.57 + 0.3 = 3.87$m

Clearly we can cross the shallow area without too much worry.

It may be that we wish to reverse this process. Being a trifle uncertain of our exact whereabouts, we wish to take a sounding and calculate the charted depth so as to be able to check this against the soundings on the chart. We merely work the other way round. Tide tables refer to ports rather than the open sea and so we shall have to estimate the appropriate height of tide using the data available. For this reason our results will not be exact. Having determined the estimated height of tide, we subtract this from the reading obtained from the echo sounder or the depth measured using the log to arrive at the charted depth.

If we wish to calculate the clearance under a bridge or other overhead obstruction we use Mean High Water Springs as our starting point. This is quoted in the port information to be found in the almanacs and on certain charts. The calculation is a trifle more complicated (see Fig 7.5).

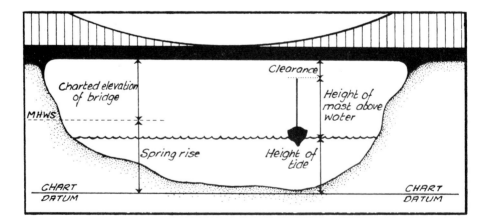

Fig 7.5 Calculating clearance below a bridge. The basic equation is: charted elevation + spring rise = height of tide + height of mast + clearance. Therefore, clearance = charted elevation + spring rise – height of tide – height of mast

Actual clearance = the charted elevation of the object
                    + spring rise
                    − actual height of tide
                    − height of mast above water

Exactly the same calculation is used to determine the height of a light above sea level at any given time except, of course, that the height of the mast is not subtracted.

We have assumed that the Duration (the time between LW and HW) is 6 hours. Whilst this is a fair enough assumption in most cases, the Duration can vary from 5 hours to 7 hours. A more accurate method of determining the actual rise at any given time is to use a tidal curve which plots the anticipated rate of rise and fall against a number of time bases to cover various durations. These are especially valuable when cruising in areas where there are unusual and pronounced variations from the normal − such as in the Solent. *The Macmillan & Silk Cut Nautical Almanac* includes such curves in the section dealing with Harbour, Coastal and Tidal Information together with a full explanation of how to use them.

So much for calculations to do with depth, we must also be able to determine horizontal tidal flows. This has already been considered in Chapter 4 although the method shown is a rule of thumb system offering a reasonably accurate figure. Again, the *Macmillan Almanac* carries a table and grid which enables one to make this calculation more accurately without additional effort. It is, however, wise to remember the system shown in Chapter 4 as this enables one to arrive at the answer without resource to any other information than the chart and the basic tide tables.

8
Weather Forecasting and Bad-weather Tactics

The reader will have noticed by now that this book is about coastal cruising and that I am defining coastal cruising as a family activity that can, and should, be enjoyed by all members of the crew. It is an activity that brings great rewards – rewards which vary from person to person – some finding them in being close to nature and away from the throb of modern life, whilst others look for the sense of satisfaction and achievement that is felt at the end of a voyage safely concluded.

Being at sea in a small boat when the weather is foul is rarely enjoyable – although there are rewards. To most folk it is uncomfortable at best and extremely frightening at worst; the rewards being granted only to those with considerable experience. The skipper who sails in conditions which are ideal from his point of view may well find that they are far too severe for his wife and children and a thoroughly frightened child can bring the whole idea of happy family cruising to an abrupt halt.

It follows, therefore, that the correct way to deal with heavy weather is to sail only when conditions are within the capacity of the weakest members of the crew. Furthermore, because accidents do happen and the skipper may find himself unable to do more than direct operations from below, the boat should not be at sea in conditions which are beyond the physical capacity of the second-in-command – usually his wife or, later perhaps, his eldest child.

Fortunately, the unexpected gale is a very rare event in the coastal waters around the United Kingdom during those months when most folk take their holidays. Talk to people who have been 'caught out in a blow' and you usually find that they have planned a strict timetable for their cruise and are determined to stick to it regardless or else they have not taken the trouble to listen to the shipping forecasts and other sources of weather information. Both are folly. The former shows many of the characteristics of those who insist on driving at 70mph in dense fog, the latter is sheer irresponsibility.

So much for gloom and doom, let us look at the various precautions that can be taken to cope with heavy weather – bearing in mind that what is a fair sailing breeze for one boat with a full and experienced crew can be a full gale for a smaller boat with a young family aboard. First, however, we should look at the forecasting services available.

Weather Forecasts

The weather around our coasts follows certain patterns but these are extremely complex thanks to the fact that the British Isles lies at what can be considered a crossroads of various weather systems. This makes forecasting far more difficult than it is in other parts of the world and the more one understands the way weather-patterns develop, the more one can read into the forecasts available. It is outside the scope of this book to cover the subject of meteorology but many others deal with it in some detail. A section of *The Macmillan & Silk Cut Nautical Almanac* is devoted to the subject and includes some excellent illustrations as well as colour photographs of typical cloud formations.

The radio is probably the most important source of information and every craft should carry at the very least a receiver which can be tuned to both the long wave and to the normal VHF frequencies. Gale warnings and forecasts for coastal waters are provided by both the BBC and the RTE (Radio Telefis Éireann) whilst the BBC transmits the standard shipping forecast covering all British home waters as well as gale warnings on, at present, long wave (200kHz – 1500m). Most of the independent radio stations situated near the coast provide forecasts for yachtsmen which cover their own coastline whilst the various Coast Radio Stations broadcast forecasts on both MF and VHF although these are available only to those who have radios covering the marine frequency bands. Full details of frequencies and times are shown in the nautical almanacs. From this it will be seen that there is no reason why the skipper should not be able to keep himself fully informed.

In addition, it is always possible to obtain advice and details of the outlook for two or three days by telephoning one of the Meteorological Offices – many of which provide a full 24-hour service. When calling these offices, explain the plan – and timing – of your movements so that they can give you the maximum assistance. Full details of these offices are printed in the almanacs.

Coastguard stations and some lighthouses make weather observations for the Meteorological Office and are usually prepared to give information about actual conditions. They will usually assist, too, by giving details of the latest weather forecast and/or gale warnings if these have been missed for any reason.

There is a lot to be said for recording weather details in the ship's

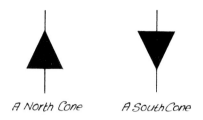

A North Cone   A South Cone

Fig 8.1 Visual gale warnings. Cones are hoisted at certain vantage points around the coast when a gale is expected within twelve hours, while the gale is blowing and during temporary lulls. North cones denote winds from north of an east/west line; south cones winds from south of that line. Some stations display three red lights in the form of a triangle at night

logbook as this improves one's awareness of changing signs and so improves one's ability to assess them and become more expert at fore-casting. This is a valuable skill as all forecasts cover fairly large areas and local conditions may be very different. Four instruments are required to do the job properly: a barometer to measure the pressure, a compass to judge wind direction, a small hand-held ventimeter to measure wind speed and a simple thermometer. Although I regret that I have never acquired this skill to any great extent, I have some friends who have become so expert that their advice is often of greater value than any other. I have a sneaking suspicion that they enjoy their cruising all the more having learnt how to read nature's signs and how best to interpret them.

Bad-weather Tactics

It is assumed that the reader is already skilled in the art of reefing and knows how to handle his craft when the weather becomes boisterous. However, no matter how much one reads about handling boats in heavy weather, there is always something to learn and a number of excellent books have been written which deal exhaustively with this subject. Some of these are listed at the end of the book. There are, however, a number of aspects of cruising during such conditions which are sometimes overlooked.

Stowage
There are two aspects to this subject. Firstly, all must be well and truly secured and secondly everything that may be required must be accessible even when the boat is being pitched about.

Some bizarre, but still serious, accidents have happened as a result of gear coming adrift and it is incredibly easy to overlook some item or other. The radio gently playing music in the background as I type this has a broken carrying-handle – a witness to just such an over-sight. It was kept stowed on a shelf by the wheel in a largish motor vessel I then owned, secured in place with a light lashing. One day, in a very moderate sea, this lashing failed and the radio fell onto the deck via the helmsman. Although neither was badly hurt, both suffered to some extent – and I learned yet another valuable lesson. Nothing can be overlooked.

All lashings should be checked periodically and again whenever bad weather is expected. It is probably best to start on the foredeck and work aft so that those items hardest to subdue when the going is rough are dealt with first. The check should, of course, extend to all areas below as well as those on deck. All rope tails should be properly stowed – there is little point in deciding to use the engine only to find that the end of the main sheet has wrapped itself around the propeller.

When all is secure, the heavy-weather gear should be overhauled so that it is ready for use if required. Storm anchors usually stowed below should be brought up on deck, shackled to their cables and lashed firmly in place (a lashing which can be cut adrift quickly with a knife is best). Storm-jibs, trysails, drogues – all the items that may be required but may well have become stowed too deeply to be pulled out rapidly – should be found and re-stowed where they can be reached without too much difficulty. In some ways the boat that avoids bad weather at all costs is at greatest risk in such times as the gear required is unlikely to have been used for some time.

Crew – Safety

This is another of those areas where there tends to be confusion between safety gear and emergency equipment. The most important single piece of gear available to keep the crew safe is the safety harness to stop anybody from going over the side (see Plate 8.1). Since such harnesses only work if they are attached to the boat at all times, jackstays must be rigged onto which the harnesses are clipped. These should be so fitted that the crew can attach themselves in the safety of the cabin and remain clipped on at all times. It is often very difficult to achieve this ideal and some re-clipping is almost always unavoidable. However, it is vital that crew can make their way out of the cockpit to the relative security of the shrouds without having to re-clip en route. At that point re-clipping is acceptable – but only if the harness is fitted with two clips – the second being attached to the shrouds or some other strong point while the first is transferred. Generally, the second clip is not as strong as the first and should not be used except when this operation is being carried out.

Emergency Gear

Whilst one would like to think that conditions will not be bad enough to require the use of such equipment, and that it is checked at

Plate 8.1   A typical safety harness (*South Western Marine Factors*)

frequent intervals on a routine basis, it is no bad thing to run down a checklist which should have been prepared and written out inside one cover of the log book. A typical list is shown in Appendix III.

One silly point to remember – against liferaft (or inflatable), see Figs 8.2, 8.3, is listed water containers. These are usually thrown over the side attached to the said inflatable by a light line. If full, they will sink. At best this means they will have to be hauled up – at worst that the line will break and they will be lost. Such water containers should never contain more than about three-quarters of their capacity. Apart from anything else, a couple of sinking water containers can seriously affect the buoyancy of the inflatable. Without wishing to be morbid, the two greatest problems facing people who have to take to an inflatable are body temperature (usually the problem of keeping warm enough in our latitudes) and thirst. Food is a very secondary requirement.

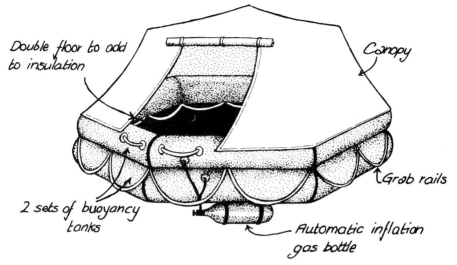

Fig 8.2 Liferaft. Liferafts should be the 'right' size. The crew provides ballast and an oversize raft is liable to be unstable

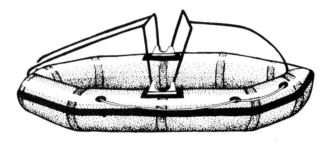

Fig 8.3 An inflatable rigged as a liferaft: (1) A canopy (use orange day-glo material) is required. A frame using the rowlocks, bow dodger support and two holes for outboard brackets as shown above can be made based on plastic tubing such as Alkathene. Large entry port aft and small one forward. (2) Rig up automatic CO_2 bottle inflation. (3) Essential stores are bailer, water, blankets, flares, first-aid kit (see text and Appendix III). A drogue may prove invaluable (use kitbag for spare clothes and blankets if necessary)

Crew – Physical State

More accidents are caused by crew failure than by gear failure. If we assume that no skipper would expose his boat to conditions too severe for it to withstand, we are left with making mistakes and insufficient physical strength as the factors most likely to cause accidents.

A tired, hungry and cold crew is an inefficient crew: decisions are taken which are clearly the wrong decisions; tempers fray, panic can set in. This way a situation which should have been only uncomfortable suddenly becomes highly dangerous.

Taking those three conditions in the above order we will start with tiredness – but that does not mean it is any more important than the other two. All are potential killers and must be treated as such.

Tiredness is not really caused by hard work as there is little continuous activity involved (as opposed to times of high activity such as during sail changes) although hard work is, of course, a factor. Much more important, however, is the strain caused by noise, by fear and by the need to hang on to something all the time. This strain is almost constant and can be extremely wearing, especially to the inexperienced.

Oddly enough, it tends to be the noise that comes as the greatest shock to those finding themselves out in a blow for the first time. It is rarely mentioned, probably because there is virtually nothing that can be done about it. There is much to be said for having children on board in the safety of a harbour during gales so that they can become attuned to the various shipboard noises before taking them to sea at all. This can be achieved by spending a few weekends on the boat at the beginning of the season when the weather is still too bad for cruising.

Fear can be reduced considerably by involving everyone in the 'pre-blow' checking and preparation. Somehow the realisation that the ship and the crew are ready, if not willing, to cope with the expected conditions helps to steady people and to make them think clearly and constructively, and clear, constructive thought is a good antidote to blind fear. As far as children are concerned, fear is more likely to be caught from their parents than from the conditions themselves. It is vital, therefore, that the adults in the party do not let their children see that they are frightened. Whilst only a fool never feels fear at sea, it should never be shown. It is far too infectious. A plentiful supply of favourite books can help to keep young minds occupied when there is nothing they can do on deck.

Much can be done to alleviate the problems of being thrown about and having to hang on. First, bunks should be made really secure. Personally, I prefer canvas lee 'boards' to anything else as they can be made high enough to work properly and can be easily dropped to give access to the bunk (see Fig 8.4). If the bottom edge of the canvas is screwed (use counter-sunk screws, large washers and eyeletted holes) to the bunk boards and the top edge is fitted with eyelets at intervals of no more than 38cm (15in), a strong piece of cord can be threaded through the top eyelets and some fastening on the underside of the deckhead – sheet fairleads are first class – and then to a simple jambing cleat. Pull tight, jamb the cord and all is snug and secure; pull the cord out of the cleat and the whole lot can be pushed down out of the way. If the bunks are a bit too wide, as is often the case with children, blankets, clothes or whatever can be folded to form a

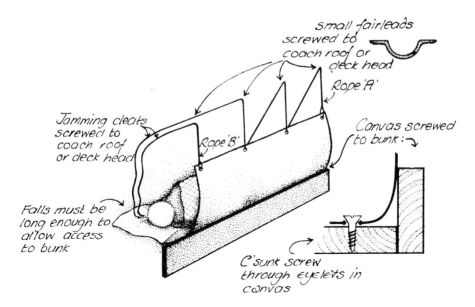

Small fairleads
screwed to
coach roof or
deck head

Rope 'A'

Jamming cleats
screwed to
coach roof
or deck head

Rope 'B'

Canvas screwed
to bunk :

Falls must be
long enough to
allow access
to bunk

C'sunk screw
through eyelets in
canvas

Fig 8.4 Canvas lee boards. They hold occupants firmly in their berths. Access can be made after releasing Rope 'B' only. All can be stowed under the mattress when not required

roll between the occupant and the ship's side. Children often prefer to stay in their bunks during a blow, and it is essential that they feel (and are) safe and secure in them.

A few canvas straps carefully positioned so that the bottom can be wedged in them while the feet are splayed out in front, thus leaving the arms and upper part of the body free to work, can work wonders. Obvious sites are the galley, the helm if wheel steering is fitted, and the chart table. A similar system can sometimes work by the mast, but it may not be possible to make such a fitting absolutely secure. If any such fitting cannot be anchored properly, it is better not to fit it at all. Any gear which is used in heavy weather must be strong enough to be used without worry.

There should be sufficient grab-handles to make hanging on a simple matter where all else fails. They should be close enough together for the smallest person on board to be able to grab hold of one before letting go of the last. If long grab-rails can be installed along the cabin so that small children can work their way along them, so much the better.

Grab-handles on deck should follow the same rule. Often there is a grab-handle running along the coachroof which is fine when working along the side decks. The problem arises that there is nothing between that grab-handle and the pulpit so that crossing the foredeck can be hazardous. Although a grab-rail running on the fore and aft line of the boat forward from the mast may interfere with the head-

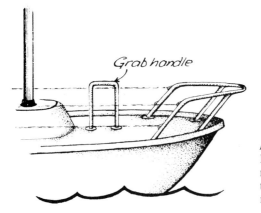

Fig 8.5 A foredeck grab handle. Like all grab handles and guard rails they must be properly bolted to the deck, using backing plates if required

sail(s) when tacking, such a rail can make the foredeck a far safer place (see Fig 8.5).

Before leaving tiredness, there is one obvious cause to be considered – lack of sleep. Many skippers take considerable pains to ensure that the rest of the crew spend sufficient time in their bunks – but take no such trouble over themselves. This is a case of inverted priorities. In most family units, it is the skipper who has the most experience and who will be needed most if things start to go wrong. He is of no value to anyone if, when that time comes, he is too tired to be effective. If anything, it is better for other members of the crew to be short of sleep. It sounds selfish but, in fact, it makes a great deal of sense. It can be very difficult to leave the helm to a less experienced person or, indeed, to leave the boat to her own devices. Nevertheless, it must be done if all the crew, including the skipper, are to get enough rest.

There are, incidentally, times when it pays to 'snug down the ship' a good deal earlier than would be the case with a full crew. Naturally, one would prefer to maintain as much drive as possible, especially if there is any risk of nearing a lee shore. However, consideration should be given to reducing sail while it is still an easy job; using the engine to provide additional power by way of compensation. It is very helpful if such evolutions as heaving-to have been tried and tested in fair weather – it is often thought that training is a bore whereas it can be great fun, so long as it is carried out in the right way without too much shouting.

Hunger and cold should be taken together as a hungry crew is often a cold crew. Apart from obvious 'iron rations' such as chocolate and a plentiful supply of sandwiches of various sorts, cake and biscuits – hot food should be available if at all possible. Cooking when the boat is being thrown about will be difficult if not impossible, but thermos flasks can be filled with hot drinks and soups. They are not frantically expensive and it is worth having as many as three or four per person on board. Since people may not be feeling at their best, each person's flasks should be filled with those things he or she likes and will most likely be able to take even when suffering from a queasy stomach. It is perfectly possible to take this thermos flask concept a stage further and buy some wide-mouthed flasks which can be filled with stew.

Incidentally, there is no need to wait for bad weather to use the flasks – everyone's life is made a lot easier if they are brought into service as a matter of course. Personally I would never dream of going on watch at night without at least two flasks of coffee ready to be broached as the mood takes me – a habit that has attracted a number of coarse comments from some of my less well-bred friends.

Clothing is, of course, important but is dealt with in Appendix I.

Suitable canvas dodgers to protect the crew on watch in the cockpit are, rightly, becoming more and more popular. They are fine allies in the fight against cold but can make it almost dangerous to climb from the cockpit to the side decks. It should be possible to remove any lashing holding such dodgers without leaving the cockpit and, if it isn't, priority should be given to changing the system.

Navigation
Whenever there is a risk of visibility becoming poor – be it as a result of fog, rain or whatever – the navigator should try to establish a fix to confirm his dead reckoning. It may be some time before another fix can be obtained and, as we shall see later, it is not always wise to rely on being able to use radio beacons etc – always assuming that the equipment required is carried on board. At the same time he should consider what harbours are available which can be entered in safety in the expected conditions, bearing in mind that it is usually safer to stay at sea than to attempt an entrance which is unknown or suspect. If time permits, he should try to build up an accurate mental picture of the area, especially that part of it that lies down wind, so that he is aware of all the dangers that might be encountered. He can then lay off a course which, whilst it may not be in the planned direction, is safe.

From then on, he has to try to maintain an accurate track. Although events do not happen that quickly at sea, it is surprising how rapidly one can find oneself in a position of no-return unless a constant, watchful eye is kept on events.

9

The Rules of the Road and Communications

All who have taken part in the racing scene, be it in dinghies or day boats, will be well aware of the vital part played by the rule book. These rules are laid down to ensure both fairness and safety. Excluding offshore racing, fairness can take priority over safety as most races are conducted in a well-disciplined group with safety boats standing by to offer assistance when required.

The cruising man is concerned only with safety and the rule book takes on a very different complexion.

Whilst the basis of this rule book remains 'The International Regulations for Preventing Collisions at Sea' many harbour and port authorities have found it necessary to impose local regulations to deal with the problems caused by modern boats and increased traffic. In addition certain countries, including the UK, have created offshore regulations which, to some extent, overrule the International Regulations. When these International Regulations were rewritten in 1972 – the new rules coming into force in 1977 – clear recognition of this need to allow local control was included in Rule 1. Previously some leeway was given under Rule 30.

It is clear, therefore, that the cruising skipper needs to have a good working knowledge of both the International Regulations and of any local rules applying to his cruising area. In practice these latter deal with such matters as Traffic Separation Zones (more on that later), traffic control within harbour limits, speed controls and regulations covering movement, anchoring and mooring – again within harbour limits. Such rules may be found in the almanacs and pilots although few publications give comprehensive details and it is wisest to check in all available sources when planning a passage. Naturally the more complex rules apply only in the busy commercial or naval ports and it is usually true to say that by keeping to waters too shallow for the larger commercial craft one can keep out of trouble. It is, however, vital that all signals regarding entry and exit through harbour mouths in such ports as Dover are thoroughly understood and obeyed.

The International Regulations

These remained unchanged for many years and most books such as this listed them in full. However, it seems likely that more frequent reviews will be made in future and so the best source is the nautical almanac which will contain the most recent rules together with, in some cases, comments on the latest interpretations of those rules. Incidentally, this is done very well in the *Macmillan & Silk Cut Nautical Almanac* which includes very helpful explanatory notes and diagrams interspersed amongst the actual rules.

The International Regulations are divided into five parts. **Part A** deals with application, responsibility and general definitions. The most important point raised in this section is that slavishly following the rules does not ensure safety but that collisions are avoided by seamanship and commonsense. Thus, no vessel is granted a total 'right of way' over all other boats but must act to avoid a collision even if such action is an apparent departure from the rules. The old couplet

> He was right, dead right, as he went along
> But now he's as dead as if he'd been wrong.

does not apply at sea; there is no 'dead right'. If you like, the rules lay down procedures to be followed whenever possible but those with the right of way still have a duty to be aware of any problems that may face the giving-way vessel and act accordingly.

Part B covers Steering and Sailing Rules and should be read in full and then the relevant passages studied with care until they are so well known that they can be applied instinctively when required.

Section I, dealing with the conduct of vessels under all conditions, emphasises the need to maintain a good look out at all times, to proceed at a safe speed, to be able to determine when a risk of collision exists and how to act when avoiding a collision, navigating in narrow channels or operating in traffic separation zones.

Many discussions heard at the club bar on a Sunday are centred on the question of commercial craft relying too heavily on radar and failing to maintain an adequate visual watch. There are, however, faults on both sides and such time could be spent more profitably considering ways that small craft could improve their own look out. For example, one often sees large low-cut headsails which obscure the helmsman's view over a wide arc ahead. This is perfectly satisfactory when the boat carries a large enough crew for one person to be responsible for keeping watch in that blind zone. It is far from satisfactory when the helmsman is the only one on watch and, under such circumstances, such a sail should not be carried even if it means using less sail area than conditions would otherwise dictate.

Unfortunately the problem doesn't stop there. On two occasions I have witnessed collisions caused by the entire crew working hard to ensure every sail was setting properly – but failing to watch where they were going. Once was with a moored boat which suffered considerable damage, the other was with a large mooring buoy which seemed indifferent to the insult.

In reduced visibility serious consideration should be given to sending a crewmember forward to maintain a watch from the foredeck; perhaps through the forehatch, as the distance gained, though short, can make a considerable difference – and not only visually as ears forward of the usual boat noises can pick up sounds of activity ahead long before they are audible to those in the cockpit.

Most cases of vessels operating at unsafe speed are linked with poor visibility. Clearly a reduction in visibility should be accompanied by a reduction in speed. It is not only the usual factors – mist, fog, rain and snow – that can impair visibility. Effective visibility at night is often reduced when near the coast or in a harbour thanks to the shore lights and great care must be taken at such times. The greatest problems are caused when car headlights sweep across the water blinding one as they pass. Incidentally, light from the cabin can have a similar effect but is, of course, easier to correct.

A boat is travelling too fast if she cannot stop or take suitable avoiding action in good time. It is rare that a sailing boat will be travelling that fast but other factors can influence the 'action time'. Thus, it is foolish to be sailing with the spinnaker set or with the boom guyed forward when visibility is poor, as both seriously increase this 'action time'. When visibility closes in, there is much to be said for handing the main if the wind is aft and running under headsails alone.

As soon as another vessel is sighted it becomes necessary to determine whether or not there is a risk of collision. This is often far harder than one would expect and the only safe way is to take a series of compass bearings at fairly frequent intervals, noting each in the log. If the bearing does not alter substantially there is a risk of collision and suitable action should be taken. Even that is not the whole story for some modern boats, especially tankers, are extremely large and a series of bearings taken on one point (eg bow at day or a light at night) can be changing considerably but there is still the danger of hitting some other part of the vessel. If that sounds ridiculous, bear in mind the fact that some tankers are well over 1,000ft long. Similar problems occur when one vessel is towing another.

When acting to avoid a collision, it is essential that whatever action is carried out is definite so that the other vessel can detect the action quickly and accurately. At night a change of course which will either show an additional navigation light or remove one from sight is best as this gives immediate and positive information to the other craft. Small course changes should be avoided as these can cause confusion.

Under most circumstances a change of course is better than a change of speed. Apart from the fact that it is almost impossible for others to detect the latter, a course change is generally safer. However, if a change of course alone will not provide sufficient margin, then it will be necessary to either reduce speed or even stop.

Making one's intentions clear becomes doubly important when one has the right of way and is making a course change either out of consideration or because it just happens that one was intended at that moment. Since the other vessel is not expecting such a change it must be made very definitely – and it is often wise to signal the intention, a subject we shall be looking at later. If the other vessel does not note your unexpected change it may well take avoiding action which will result in the risk of collision remaining and confusion. If necessary, make an exaggerated course change, hold it for a while (possibly as long as fifteen minutes) and then bear away on the required course. Many skippers of small boats are prepared to give way to commercial craft in most circumstances. One might twist the old adage and say 'consideration must not only be done but must be seen to be done'.

The draughtsmen of the International Regulations would seem to have had some difficulty when drawing up Rule 9 which deals with narrow channels. One is inclined to sympathise with them. No attempt is made to define a narrow channel – presumably any area where vessels are unable to navigate freely as a result of their draught is covered by the rule. However, small vessels are defined as being under 20m in length in Rule 9(b) though many areas used by cruising folk include channels which impose serious limitations on boats considerably smaller than that.

The rules themselves are straightforward – all vessels are obliged to keep as close to the starboard side of the channel as possible and small craft must not impede the passage of vessels which can navigate safely only within the channel. Sailing boats should take special care when tacking across the channel to avoid causing an obstruction and anchoring within the channel is allowed only in an emergency.

Although it would seem that the regulations do not cover smaller channels it is commonsense to abide by the rule in these areas as well, as far as possible. However, there is an additional hazard often encountered in such an area which may well turn the rule on its head. That hazard is the novice sailor. Many estuary areas with tidal channels make fine 'nursery slopes' and many novice sailors may well be too engrossed – or too ignorant – to notice that they are creating problems. In these cases I suggest that experience should give way unless it is dangerous so to do; after all, we were all novices once.

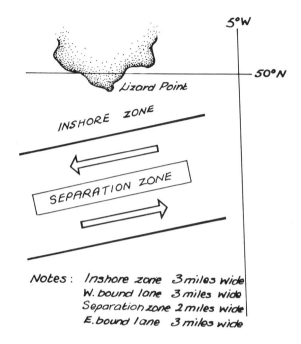

Notes : Inshore zone 3 miles wide
         W. bound lane 3 miles wide
         Separation zone 2 miles wide
         E. bound lane 3 miles wide

Fig 9.1 A typical traffic separation scheme. Modern charts show above and details are given in almanacs. Such schemes are subject to alteration from time to time and charts should be corrected when changes are announced in *Notices to Mariners* and almanac supplements (issued in July each year)

There are a number of Traffic Separation Schemes in operation around the coasts of the UK (Fig 9.1 shows a typical scheme). These are essential to the safe working of large, fast commercial vessels operating in confined waters. They are, frankly, a problem for the small-boat user, especially the small sailing-boat user, and there is no doubt that the best course of action is to avoid these schemes if possible. Generally it is possible to use the Inshore Traffic Zone which is perfectly permissible although care should be taken to keep clear of the boundary line between this zone and the first lane.

Under no circumstances should one travel along a lane in the wrong direction. Although permitted it is probably unwise to tack against the wind along a lane as there is a clear duty placed on sailing craft to avoid impeding vessels using the traffic lanes and tacking to and fro across the lane could make it difficult to fulfil this duty.

The separation zones can be likened to the central reservation of a dual carriageway; they are there to separate traffic and must not be used for any other purpose except in an emergency. If a Traffic Separation Zone must be crossed, this should be carried out at right angles. Not only does this reduce the time taken to clear the Scheme but it offers the largest profile to those watching from the bridges of other vessels. It is wise to use both power and sail so as to complete

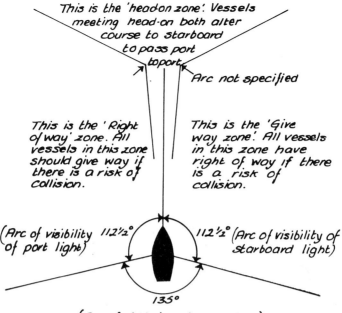

Fig 9.2 Right of way when two power-driven vessels meet

Table 9.1 The 'Give Way' Order

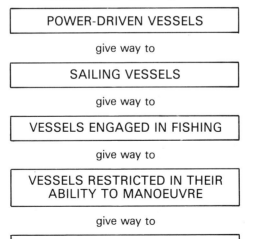

Note: This does not apply in narrow channels, in Traffic Separation Schemes or when vessels are overtaking

this manoeuvre as quickly as possible. It is even wiser to give all Traffic Separation Schemes a very wide berth.

Although a sailing boat (or a craft of under 20m) would be infringing the rules if it were to impede a larger craft using the correct traffic lane, should a risk of collision occur the usual rules apply and the craft wrongly creating the problem can become the craft with the right of way. One would like to think that this is of academic interest only.

Section II deals with the conduct of vessels in sight of one another – the 'Rule of the Road' as it is generally understood. Fig 9.2, Table 9.1 and Fig 9.3 summarise these rules. There are, however, a couple of points to note.

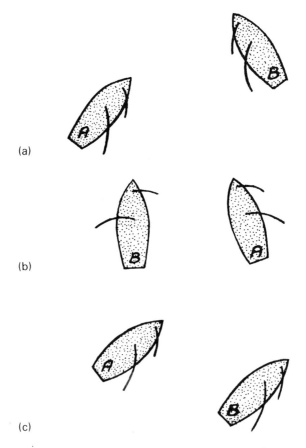

(a)

(b)

(c)

Fig 9.3   Right of way when two sailing vessels meet: 'A' gives way to 'B'
(a) A sailing boat with the wind on the port side gives way to one with the wind on the starboard side
(b) It is the position of the mainsail which determines right of way. 'A' still gives way even if 'B' is sailing by the lee
(c) The windward boat gives way to the leeward when both are on the same tack

Any sailing craft with its engine running is deemed to be a vessel under power whether or not any sails are set.

A vessel engaged in fishing, a vessel restricted in her ability to manoeuvre and a vessel not under command should show the required signals – shapes by day and lights by night. In practice, of course, not all bother to display these signals – especially fishing boats – and, although the regulations do not make it clear who is then responsible, commonsense dictates that 'if in doubt – keep clear and give way'. The signals used are shown below under Communications.

Section III consists of a single rule concerning the conduct of vessels in restricted visibility. The rule applies to all vessels whether or not there is another vessel in sight or known to be in the area. Basically it emphasises the need to proceed at a safe speed and to be ready to reduce speed even further, or stop if necessary, and to make rapid course changes. From the sailing point of view these can be fulfilled only if the rig is snugged down, ie no spinnakers, large cruising chutes or boom guys etc.

Parts C and D look at the various signals relating to preventing collisions, which are considered under Communications below. **Part E** covers certain exemptions which allow time for the changes required by the new regulations to be carried out; certain of these exemptions have already expired.

Communications

This subject can be divided into three parts. Firstly there are those lights, shapes and sound signals required under Parts C and D of the International Regulations which, broadly speaking, tell others what you are, what you are doing and what you intend to do. Secondly there is the International Code which enables messages to be passed even when there is no common language using either flags or morse code. Rarely required, this subject receives far less attention than it deserves simply because if it is needed at all it will be needed urgently. Finally there is the question of clear voice communication using radio. This is becoming more widespread as the cost of suitable equipment becomes more favourable.

If we take a further look at Fig 9.2 and Table 9.1 we can see that the right of way depends on the type of craft, the direction of travel and its ability to manoeuvre. By day the first two factors are usually obvious (the usual exception being the sailing craft with sails set and engine running). Shapes are used, hung in the rigging, to cover the third factor (see Table 9.2). By night, however, lights must be used to cover all the required information and four basic types are used in a variety of combinations. These basic types are as follows – see Fig 9.2 for a diagram of the various arcs of visibility specified for each type:

1 *Sidelights*   Visible from right ahead to 22½° abaft the appropriate beam (112½° total arc); the port light is red and the starboard light green. These lights are usually positioned at low level, in the rigging, on coachroofs, on superstructure or on pulpits.

2 *Masthead lights*   White lights visible from right ahead to 22½° abaft both beams (225° total arc); they cover the same arc as both the sidelights. These lights must be mounted over the fore and aft centreline of the vessel at a reasonable distance above the gunwhale and are usually mounted on the mast although not necessarily at the masthead despite the name. When a vessel is required to carry two masthead lights, the after one will be substantially higher than the one forward.

3 *Sternlights*   White lights visible from right aft to 22½° abaft both beams (135° total arc); these lights complete the circle. They are mounted at low level as near the stern as possible. Vessels when towing carry a towing light covering the same arc. This is a yellow light carried higher than the normal sternlight.

4 *All-round lights*   Visible, as the name implies, throughout an unbroken arc of 360°; they are carried in the rigging where they can be best seen. When such lights are specified they are rigged one above the other and, in the case of three lights, equally spaced.

Table 9.2 lists the lights and shapes we are likely to require. These should be memorised. A complete list of all lights and shapes is shown in the International Regulations and it is worth reading through them although, luckily for us, there is no need to commit them all to memory. This is because, as cruising folk, we shall be either a power vessel or a sailing vessel and have a duty to give way to and keep clear of all other craft. For once, then, we can indulge ourselves in some gross simplification. With the exception of the nine light combinations shown below, the message is always the same: if there is a risk of collision it is our job to give way. Let us look at the combinations that demand rather greater thought.

1 *A single white light*   Slightly worrying, a single white light can be a number of things including a masthead light giving us advance warning of almost any vessel. It can be an anchor light, the light of a small craft or the sternlight of any vessel (in which case we are in its 'overtaking zone').

Lights carried on small vessels are usually of low intensity and are fairly close when first spotted – masthead lights are more powerful and are first seen at a distance.

Action: check whether or not a risk of collision exists. If it does, act as if the light is a sternlight until – and if – proved wrong. This means give way and keep clear whilst keeping an open mind on the situation – it may be a little dinghy about to change course and cause further problems!

2 *A single sidelight (red or green)* OR

3 *A single sidelight (red or green) and red over green above* OR

4 *Both sidelights (red and green)* OR

5 *Both sidelights (red and green) and red over green above*   In all cases we are looking at a sailing craft. If we are under power we must give way. If we too are under sail, we must try to determine which boat has right of way (see Fig 9.3) and act accordingly. If there is any doubt as to which has right of way we shall assume it is our duty to give way and keep clear.

6 *A white light and red over green above*   This is a sailing boat and we are in its 'overtaking zone'. We give way and keep clear whether under power or under sail.

7 *A red sidelight with either one or two white lights above*   This is a vessel under power and we are in its 'right of way zone'. If we are under power and there is a risk of collision we must give way and keep clear. If we are under sail we have the right of way but it may not be wise to insist upon it (see below).

8 *A green sidelight with either one or two white lights above*   This is a vessel under power and we are in its 'give way zone' and so have the right of way whether under power or sail. We shall maintain our speed and course and await developments with interest (but see below).

9 *Both sidelights and either one or two white lights above*   This is a vessel under power and we are in its 'head on zone'. If we are under power and there is a risk of collision we shall change course to starboard. If we are wise this course change will be large enough to remove the risk of collision even if the other vessel fails to take similar avoiding action. If we are sailing we have right of way (but see below).

These nine combinations should be learned by heart.

Table 9.2   Lights and Shapes required for Cruising Craft

LIGHTS

A power-driven vessel under way shall carry
*Sidelights
*2 white masthead lights
*Sternlight

It is advisable for all power-driven vessels to carry these lights if possible but the regulations allow

Power-driven vessels under 50m need carry only
*Sidelights
*1 white masthead light
*Sternlight

Power-driven vessels under 7m and with a maximum speed of 7 knots need carry only
*1 white all-round light
*Sidelights (if possible)

A sailing vessel under way shall carry
*Sidelights
*Sternlight
*In addition two all-round lights at the masthead – red over green – may be carried

The regulations allow the following exceptions for small craft

Vessels under 12m may carry
*A single lantern combining the above lights at or near the masthead

Vessels under 7m may carry
*A white light 'which shall be exhibited in sufficient time to prevent a collision'

Notes Obviously the more light carried the better the chances of being seen. The best combination would be sidelights, sternlight and the two all-round lights if that was the only consideration. However, electricity is sometimes a problem on sailing boats in which case the combined lantern has two advantages. It uses only one bulb and is easier to see than normal sidelights when the boat is heeled. It must not be used with the all-round lights. If a combined lantern is fitted the normal lights must be carried as well (they are needed when under power and, in any case, may be needed if the masthead bulb fails) so there is no saving in capital outlay. Whilst the last rule is adequate for a dinghy that happens to be out after dark all cruising boats should be fitted with proper navigation lights.

A vessel at anchor shall exhibit
*An all-round white light near the bow

A vessel aground shall exhibit
*An all-round white light near the bow and two all-round red lights

Note These two instructions apply to vessels up to 50m. Above that additional lights are required, and many commercial craft show their deck working/cargo lights when at anchor.

SHAPES

Shapes are used during daylight hours under the following circumstances

A vessel at anchor shall exhibit
*A ball near the bow

A vessel aground shall exhibit
*Three balls in a vertical line

A sailing vessel under sail when also under power
*A conical shape, apex downward

Notes A vessel of under 7m need not show the appropriate shape or light provided that she is clear of any channel, fairway or anchorage. Although very few sailing boats bother to show the shape indicating that they are under both sail and power (and very few people writing on this subject even bother to mention the provision) it is helpful to fellow sailing men if the regulation is followed. One can understand a reluctance to bother for the sake of, say, large commercial craft but this provision is aimed to assist people like us.

Shapes can be manufactured from two pieces of plywood slotted together or can be inflatable – the latter are available from most chandlers.

The power of the lights carried in larger vessels is far greater than that of those on smaller craft. If we see combinations 7, 8 or 9 with two white lights it is reasonable to assume that it is a larger vessel and that we have noticed her long before she has noticed us. Add to this the fact that the bows of a large vessel obscure quite a large area of the vessel's 'head on zone' from its bridge and it ceases to be sensible to assume that ones presence has been noticed at all. This is especially true when we are sailing as we shall be heeling or rolling making it even harder to see our lights. To depend on the other ship's radar is folly, even if we carry a suitable radar reflector which is an essential item of equipment. The wisest course for us to take is the one that will remove us from any risk of collision as quickly as possible and it is safe to make that course change even if the regulations suggest we should maintain direction and speed as it is unlikely that we will have been spotted early enough for such a change to cause confusion.

As we have already noted, any other combination of lights means we must give way. Fig 9.4 shows the safest courses to take in various situations but assumes that one knows the direction of travel of the vessel with the right of way. To determine this we must try to decide whether or not we can see any sidelights – not always as easy as it sounds when faced with a number of lights to be identified. If we can see the red sidelight, both sidelights or no sidelights at all – the best change is to starboard. If we can see only the green sidelight, we should turn to port. These changes will take us around the stern or clear to starboard. Remember that some of the large vessels and tows one encounters are very long indeed and the turns must be sufficient to clear their sterns.

Sound signals, some of which can be made using a lamp as well as sound, fall into two sections – those which inform others of our intentions and those which warn of our presence in restricted visibility. Basically three types of sound-producing equipment are required to comply with all the regulations: a whistle (or hooter), a bell and a gong. Vessels under 12m are not required to carry the gong. Many of the hooters and bells carried by small craft are inadequate; remember they have to be heard by those on the bridge of a large vessel against a fair amount of background noise. A 'short blast' should last about 1sec and a 'long blast' about 4sec; intervals between blasts should be about 1sec, whilst intervals between signals should be 10sec.

A vessel wishing to indicate a manoeuvre to another uses the following code:

1 short blast = I am altering course to starboard
2 short blasts = I am altering course to port
3 short blasts = I am running my engines astern

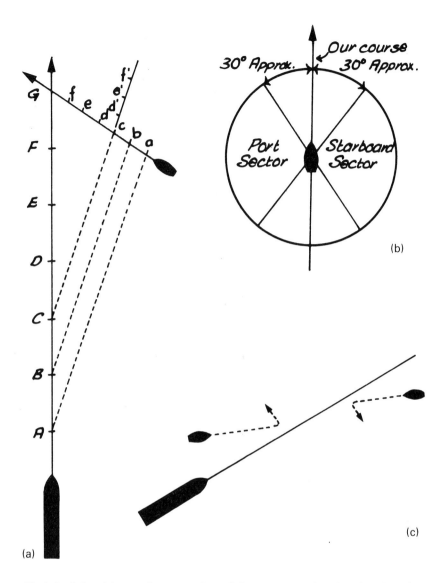

Fig 9.4 Safest 'give way' courses: One of the most worrying situations is to be the Right of Way vessel when the Give Way vessel is a considerably larger and faster craft such as a large merchantman.

According to the International Regulations we should maintain our course and speed. However, experience shows that many such merchantmen either fail to see smaller craft or else decide to ignore the rules and just keep going. It follows that, sooner or later, we must decide what we shall do if the other vessel fails to give way.

Consider Fig 9.4(a) for a moment. The merchantman on course A–G is spotted when we are at *a*. We take a bearing and note it in the log. Fifteen minutes later, when we are at *b*, we take a further bearing which, as it is the same, indicates that a risk of collision exists. After a further fifteen minutes has passed and we have reached *c*, we repeat the exercise and confirm the risk.

Since the merchantman has made no apparent move to change course, we have a decision to take. Do we continue to maintain our course or do we not? Although the

International Regulations clearly suggest that we just plough on, experience indicates that this is unwise. If we continue and the merchantman also maintains her course, all we shall achieve is to reduce the distance between the two vessels – we decide to change course.

Now, if we have not been seen – or if it has been decided to ignore us – almost any change of course is safe and will take us away from danger. However, it is quite possible that we have been seen and that the helm of the merchantman has been put over already – many large vessels can run for a considerable distance after helm has been applied before we, in a small boat, would be able to detect any change of course. What we cannot know, of course, is what new course has been ordered and so there is the real risk that our new course may combine with her new course to continue a risk of collision. We can, however, reduce the dangers should this happen.

During daylight

During daylight, the best way to reduce the danger is to increase the reaction time available to make a further correction. To do this we must turn so that our stern is pointing at the merchantman – ie follow the line *c–d'–e'*. At the same time there is merit in hoisting the International Code flag 'E' which means 'I am turning to starboard'.

This holds good if the other vessel is in either the port or starboard sectors as shown on Fig 9.4(b) and we have the right of way (in part of the starboard sector this would apply only if we are under sail).

When the angle between the courses of the two vessels is very small, this action leaves us far too close to the other vessel's track, assuming she maintains her course. Instead, there comes a point when it is far wiser to turn so that our new course is away from and at right angles to the assessed track of the merchantman – bearing in mind that it is far from easy to assess the track. This is shown in Fig 9.4(c). Whilst this does not achieve the maximum possible reaction time it is a good compromise between achieving this ideal and keeping well clear.

At night

The most important factor at night is to tell the watchkeeper on the merchantman that one has given way as quickly as possible. This is achieved by showing him the green starboard sidelight. Naturally, the course selected will be the one that creates the maximum reaction time whilst keeping the green light presented – and this applies regardless of the relative position of the merchantman.

Using a white flare

It is often suggested that a white flare should be shown to indicate one's presence in such situations. Those who have tried report that the usual reaction is for the other vessel to change course towards the flare – one presumes this is because they are not sure what is meant and are coming to investigate. It is, therefore, probably unwise to use such a flare except as an extreme measure.

Shining a torch on the sails may well help although it is not as easy to see as one might think. Easier to see is a powerful white light trained on the bridge of the other vessel but the problem is that it is extremely difficult to keep such a light trained on the bridge and it may become obscured by the crests of the waves. In either case it can look like a signalling lamp and, since the flashes will be random, there is the risk that, once again, the merchantman will come over to investigate

These signals can be given using a light in which case it should be an all-round white light although if only one vessel is in sight a normal signalling lamp or torch can be used. It is often helpful if a proposed manoeuvre is signalled and almost essential if a small vessel is going to give way to a larger one out of consideration as such a move may be contrary to the regulations despite the fact that it is most helpful. Note too that the 3 short blasts indicate that the engine is running astern and not that the vessel is making stern way. It can take quite a long time from the moment the engines are put astern before a large vessel will stop, let alone make stern way.

It is only good manners to request permission to overtake when in a channel or fairway. The signals used in this situation are:

2 long + 1 short blast = I intend to overtake to starboard
2 long + 2 short blasts = I intend to overtake you to port

The vessel about to be overtaken indicates agreement by giving 1 long + 1 short + 1 long + 1 short blast.

Any vessel in doubt about either the intentions of another vessel or about the effectiveness of the action being taken indicates these doubts by giving 5 short blasts. Naturally, this is a signal used only when there is a risk of collision and by the vessel with the right of way. It may, however, be used by a vessel about to be overtaken if her master considers it unsafe for the vessel astern to carry out this intention (this is a special case of a vessel with the right of way using the signal when there is a risk of collision so does not conflict with the general rule).

So much for the manoeuvring signals. A far more common need is the sound signal for use in poor visibility. Full details are shown in the almanac and it is probably unnecessary to learn them by heart.

It may happen that one merely wishes to attract the attention of someone – perhaps to invite them aboard for a drink. The regulations state quite clearly that any such signals must be easily distinguished from any of the authorised signals shown above or any other signal specified in the International Regulations. Above all, they must be easily distinguished from the distress signals which we shall be looking at next. When at sea the best signal for drawing attention is a white flare – this can also be used to attract the attention of the watch on a large vessel if there is a risk of collision and, for any reason, you cannot take avoiding action.

Distress signals must be used only when there is immediate and serious danger. A complete list is shown in Annex IV of the International Regulations, but the following are appropriate to cruising vessels:

A continuous signal using the hooter   This should be in the form of a succession of the letters SOS in Morse to avoid any confusion (ie ···---··· ···---···).

The same signal made by a flashing light is effective at night. An all-round white light installed for signalling purposes, is ideal.

The MAYDAY procedure used on VHF radio (this will be dealt with later).

The International Code signal NC which can be made using flags or by Morse (but it is better to use SOS when using Morse, one is less likely to make errors).

Any square flag flown either above or below a ball   The ensign can be adjusted to make it square and one should be carrying a suitable shape for use when anchoring.

A red flare, either hand-held or of the parachute type. The parachute flare has a greater range than the hand-held type. Best system is to let off two or three parachute flares at intervals of about five minutes (don't worry, if anyone has seen the first or it has been reported to the coastguard as a 'possible', someone will be looking out for the second but it may take them time to get into position, hence the long delay between flares). As soon as you have reason to believe you have been spotted, use hand flares to give an accurate position. These flares are the most effective visual signal at night, far less so by day.

A smoke signal giving off orange smoke   Very effective by day unless there is a strong wind blowing.

Also listed is the arm signal made by slowly raising and lowering the arms to each side of the body. The snag is that many people just do not recognise this and may even wave back: don't laugh, it has happened! Those ignorant of the sea are more likely to report a red flare and, if you are close enough for them to see your arms, you are close enough for a flare to work, even in daylight.

International Code of Signals

The basis for the International Code of Signals will be found in a publication of that title obtainable from HM Stationery Office. The signals provide for communication where there is no common language and can be transmitted by flag, by flashing light or sound signal using the Morse code, by voice using the international phonetic alphabet or by any other available means. The code falls into three groups:

Single-letter signals which are either urgent or commonly required
Two-letter signals for less urgent signals
Three-letter signals beginning with the letter M. These deal with medical matters

In addition to these groups there are a number of Tables of Complements numbered 0 to 9. Thus K (I wish to communicate with you) can carry a number to give further detail. So K4 becomes 'I wish to communicate with you by Morse signalling lamp' as the other possibilities 'by south' and 'by fire fighting appliance' are clearly nonsensical.

Although most signals are complete using the letter code, some take a figure suffix. CB – 'I require immediate assistance' – can be more specific as CB4 – 'I require immediate assistance, I am aground'. Similarly BR(4) reads 'I require a helicopter urgently (with a doctor).

Obviously one must have the code book to make the fullest possible use of the system but most folk rely on the almanacs which list the signals most likely to be required. They also give details of the flags associated with the code and instructions on procedure. Naturally none of this helps if one is on the receiving end and cannot decode the messages being transmitted but it is unlikely that one would require the full code book whilst cruising around the UK.

One final point before leaving this subject is that great care must be taken when sending International Code signals to avoid confusion with those laid down in the International Regulations. Thus, B (_...) transmitted using the hooter could mean 'I am taking in, or discharging, or carrying dangerous goods' (International Code) or 'I am being towed' (International Regulations). Others, such as S, mean the same in both – 'I am operating astern propulsion'. R (._.), which is used in poor visibility to draw special attention to a vessel has no meaning in the International Code to avoid confusion.

It is expensive to carry a full set of International Code flags but it costs nothing to learn and practice the Morse code. This should be understood by all cruising men as it can be used to communicate with HM ships, most merchant navy ships (of any nationality if the International Code is used), coastguards, pilots and port authorities. To be proficient one has to keep in practice and there is no better way than to rig up a system so that members of the family can 'chat' together in Morse – it comes surprisingly quickly. One fringe advantage is that one can communicate with ones spouse in public places by squeezing a hand and be assured that nobody else will intercept the message!

However, at the end of the day the simplest way to communicate, subject to sharing a common language, is by speech. This brings us into the realm of radio which is dealt with in the next chapter. There are times when a radio is inappropriate and then a loud hailer can be a great blessing. If a Tannoy type seems a bit extravagant think in terms of a good old-fashioned speaking trumpet.

10
Radio and Electronic Aids

All boats should carry a receiving radio capable of picking up the various shipping and coastal weather forecasts mentioned in Chapter 8. In some places reception is not good and music lovers, be they of a classical inclination or followers of the pop charts, will probably want this piece of equipment to include a tape recorder. If so, a spare set of batteries should be kept hidden away as the tape deck uses a great deal of power and it is not just annoying to find the batteries are flat when the time comes to listen to the shipping forecast.

Transmitting Radios

As far as cruising around the coast is concerned, the only ones of interest are the ones operating in the VHF marine bands. Under normal conditions these will have a range of 10/20 miles but can sometimes exceed that figure by a considerable amount.

A licence must be obtained before such a radio is used and both it and the installation will have to be inspected before this licence is issued. It is usually wise to employ a reputable company to install the radio and its aerial as this will ensure maximum performance and that the inspection will pass without difficulty. Once issued, this licence will be renewed each year so long as the licence fee is paid in time. If it is not, a new application must be made which means a further inspection.

It is not only the installation that must be approved. All licensed radios with a transmitting facility other than certain types designed to provide emergency distress signals must be under the control of a person holding a Restricted Certificate of Competence. This certificate is available to any British (or British Commonwealth) national who can satisfy the examiner that he knows how to operate the radio, the correct procedure to use and how to keep the required radio log. The requirements are pretty basic and the prospect of having to take the test need not deter anyone considering a VHF installation. The authorities fully appreciate that such installations improve safety and do all in their power to assist candidates. Once granted, the certificate remains valid for life.

With the many thousands of sets in operation around our waters, it

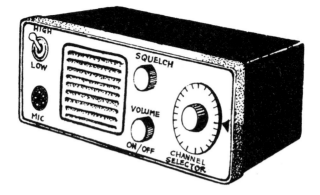

Fig 10.1 Typical marine-band VHF radio. Modern units of this sort are very simple having only five controls: an on/off and volume control, the channel selector (with up to 50 channels depending on the model), a transmitting switch on the microphone, a high/low switch to control output and the squelch control used to control background noise

is obvious that all must obey the rules if chaos is not to rule supreme.

The nautical almanacs give basic details of the procedures to be followed and full details are to be found in the *Handbook for Radio Operators* and *Notices to Ship Wireless Stations*, copies of which should be carried if a radio is installed.

Apart from the safety aspects of carrying a radio, it greatly simplifies communications with harbour and port authorities and enables one to obtain advice from HM Coastguard as well as up-to-date local forecasts. A typical unit is shown in Fig 10.1. At the time this is being written (April 1982) there is little change out of £300 by the time the equipment has been purchased and installed and the required licences obtained.

CB Radio

Radios working on the Citizens' Band – rigs, as they are called – are no substitute for the Marine Band radio. However, they have uses when used alongside their official cousins.

The one drawback with marine radios is that ship-to-shore calling is not allowed unless routed through one of the coastal radio stations – a rather formal and expensive proceeding. Likewise, there are restrictions on using them in harbours and this, added to the costs involved in carrying a second, hand-held radio, effectively rules out the possibility of using it to provide ship-to-dinghy communications. CB radio, with its much lower costs and few restrictions, make both possible. A pair of radios can be obtained for under £200 and enable one to talk to the children when they are off in the dinghy – a great worry eliminator – and to do so quite legally whether they remain afloat or go ashore. There are no tests to consider and procedures are very much slacker than when considering marine bands, the only restriction being the need to carry a valid licence presently costing £10 per annum.

Although, in an emergency, one could often contact someone ashore using CB, the odds are that that person would have no knowledge of the marine rescue services and the position could become very difficult. With considerable luck one might contact another sailor who also carried a marine-band radio and would be able to act as a relay station. From this it can be seen that CB is no replacement for a proper VHF radio. It could be argued that any radio is better than none at all and I would agree that a CB radio should be carried if one just cannot afford to buy a proper marine radio – but I would strongly suggest that all available pennies should go into a piggy bank to rectify the situation as soon as possible.

Electronic Aids

There are many different forms of electronic aid available on the market today from cheap Radio Direction Finders (RDF) to highly complex systems such as the Decca Navigator, and from radar sets to sailing efficiency meters. Personally, I see them as a great aid to the experienced and a bit of a menace to the novice. I will justify this by saying that all the novices I know who first went to sea with RDF or some other navigational system have, as a result, never acquired the navigational skills they would need should something go wrong with their 'little black boxes'.

RDF has its uses and can be a great blessing in poor visibility. The system is very simple. A radio receiver with a directional aerial is adjusted to the wavelength of a beacon in the area which is sending out a signal. This signal includes an identification code in Morse so that the operator knows which station is being monitored. By rotating the aerial – or the entire radio in the case of those with an integral aerial – the signal will drop away when that aerial is correctly aligned with the radio waves coming from the beacon. This is called the 'null'. Having found the null point, a bearing can be read either from an integral compass within the unit or, in the case of separate aerials, by checking the angle the aerial is making with the boat's centreline – exactly as one reads a pelorus – and applying this figure to the reading from the steering compass.

Given two or three good bearings taken in this fashion, one has a fix – if all has gone according to plan. The problem is that it is often far from easy to obtain a good 'null' and one has to contend with a wide arc which produces no signal. This means that one has to assess the null point by checking either side of the null and taking the average. On top of that, many different factors can affect the radio

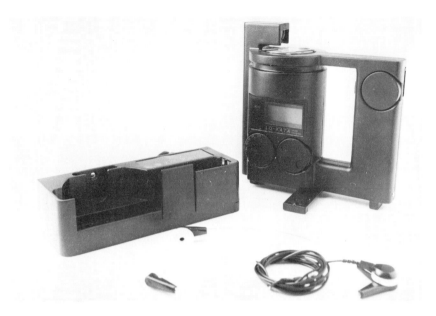

Plate 10.1   RDF unit by Lo-Kata Ltd. The required beacon frequency is set and is displayed in the panel above the controls. Earphones assist in identifying the beacon signal which is repeated by the flashing null light on handle. Volume is adjusted by control on handle. Rotate until both sound signal and null light fade. Read off bearings from compass. Can be used for taking visual bearings as well as radio bearings and will receive BBC Long Wave for shipping forecasts. Storage is in special base bracket which includes battery charger

wave coming from the beacon so that it no longer runs true. These errors cannot be eliminated no matter how good the equipment carried may be or how experienced the operator. The two main factors are the coastline and electrical storms. No bearing should be taken if the radio waves are running near to and roughly parallel with the shore – it is better to choose another beacon even if it is at extreme range.

Having said all that, if it is used only as a check to the more traditional methods of navigation or as a poor visibility aid, the RDF system has much to commend it and, being fairly cheap to buy, most folk will wish to carry a suitable receiver.

Incidentally, one can obtain radios which will pick up all the usual BBC and commercial radio stations and which include a RDF feature. If one is thinking of purchasing a new receiver for the boat, it is well worth considering one that combines both functions.

As to the other electronic aids, I feel that details of them would be out of place in this book as they are of use only to those who are cruising further afield or who are interested in racing. If the reader wishes to learn more, I would refer him to the books mentioned in the Bibliography.

11
Services

The cruising boat, like any other home, must provide all the services required – heating, lighting, cooking, waste disposal and so on.

Electricity

'Since batteries were first used for marine purposes, there has been one type readily available to yachtsmen. This is known as the fully discharged or flat battery.' Thus does John French open the chapter dealing with batteries and charging equipment in his excellent text book *Electrics and Electronics for Small Craft*.

These batteries remain readily available and one of the aspects of cruising which can easily become a constant source of worry is the need to generate and store electricity. Even the cruising man who avoids using any more electricity than he must – and the demand can be kept very small as we shall see – must at least rely on it for his navigation lights as the older, and more romantic, oil lamps do not meet the specifications now laid down in the International Regulations.

Our first task must be to calculate and analyse our demand and this should be done as accurately as possible without falsely lowering the estimated figures if we are to avoid trouble later on. In Table 11.1 we see a typical cruising boat's equipment and power consumption. At this stage we want to use watt hours – simply the number of watts consumed by each piece of equipment multiplied by the hours it will be in use each day. Where the equipment is of a known wattage, this is easy. If, however, the figure known is the current consumed, we must multiply this by the voltage of the system to find the watts (ie watts = amps × volts).

From the table we can see how a fairly normal installation can create a demand as high as 1,066 watt hours per day. To give some idea of the implications of such a demand – this could mean running the auxiliary for up to five hours a day to keep the battery well charged. If we intend to run the 'iron topsail' for that sort of time each day we have no problems. However, not all cruising men rely that heavily on the engine and some use outboard motors with no inherent charging facility. We can, of course, use a separate generator but this could mean running it for anything from five to ten hours a day depending on its output. Few of us would wish to ruin perfect sailing days by having an engine chattering away purely to provide us with electricity – and to provide it very inefficiently. The first rule states, therefore, the electrical demand on a sailing boat should be kept as small as possible.

Table 11.1   Typical Electrical Demand for a Cruising Boat

Equipment	Av daily use in hours	Total watts installed	Av watt hours per day
Navigation lights: 4 lamps of 12 watts	5	48	240
Compass lights: 2 lamps of 3.5 watts	5	7	35
Chart table light: 3.5 watts	2	3.5	7
Spreader lights: 2 lamps of 12 watts	1	24	24
Cabin lights: 5 lamps of 12 watts	6	60	360
Radio, echo sounder, navigational aids and miscellaneous equipment			400*
			1,066

*This figure varies a good deal depending on exactly what equipment is installed and how it is powered (eg many echo sounders can use their own dry batteries)

Let us take a further look at Table 11.1 and see what we can do. For a start, it should be noted that we should require only three of our navigation lights when sailing so we can show a saving of 12 watts. However, we can do better than that. If we use a masthead combination lamp with a single bulb of 25 watts we end up with a total demand of 125 watt hours – a saving of 115 watt hours. This is adequate for general sailing and we must have the other lights installed for when we are under power so there is nothing to stop us switching to the individual lights if we feel that we are more likely to be seen. (To achieve this we should include the all-round red and green lights at the masthead; this puts up demand again but they would be used only in the proximity of other craft). We can use an alternative form of cabin lighting – we shall look at that later – and so save another 360 watt hours.

The other large figure covers a number of items. Although buying electricity in the form of dry batteries is the most expensive way to buy it, there is much to be said for powering as many of the navigational items as possible with dry batteries – and using them only when required. By so doing and by taking care to switch off unwanted equipment, it should be possible to reduce this figure by half to 200 watt hours; but that would mean not using such luxuries as electric pumps on the fresh-water system and reverting to hand pumps.

We have reduced the demand to about 400 watt hours – a much more reasonable figure – but we still have to generate that power and store it. Having accepted the need for batteries, the next question to consider is what sort and what size. In addition to the above power requirements we shall have to take into consideration the power needed to start the engine assuming it to be fitted with electric starting. The manufacturer's handbook usually specifies the required size, giving this in ampere hours. This defines the storage capacity of the battery and normally applies to the 10-hour rate. Thus, a 90AH battery should sustain a discharge of 9 amps for 10 hours. This is the sort of size we would expect to start a typical diesel. Now, it can be rather important that there is a properly charged battery always available to start the engine and so it makes a great deal of sense to install two – one for services and one for engine starting only.

If we divide the daily demand in watt hours by the voltage of the system, we arrive at a figure (in ampere hours) which gives us the size of battery required for service duties. Thus, the demand of 1,066 watt hours would require an 88AH battery if the system is run on 12 volts. Having said that, battery failure is not unknown and there is a strong case for having both large enough to handle engine starting. For this reason, I have two 125AH batteries installed although the service demand is under 400 watt hours, a demand that could be met by a 35AH battery. This has the added advantage that daily recharging is not required as the battery, when fully charged, will last for four days if necessary.

When two batteries are installed into the same charging circuit, it is essential that some method is included to stop one from draining the other. This is achieved by using blocking diodes – which can be thought of as simple one-way valves – and the circuit shown in Fig 11.1 is the system usually employed, although there are other ways of achieving the same objective.

Having determined the size of the battery or batteries we have to decide which type to buy. There are two basic types available – the well-known lead/acid type as used in cars and the alkaline type. Thanks to the number of lead/acid batteries made to service the automobile industry, these are considerably cheaper than their alkaline brothers. Alkaline batteries do have a number of advantages, not least that they can be left unattended for long periods without losing charge. As so often, the choice depends on the cash available. However, if lead/acid is chosen, the battery must be suited to marine duties and the temptation to purchase cheaper units intended for land applications should be avoided.

Whichever type is fitted, the installation is important. Firstly, batteries must be checked and maintained at frequent intervals if problems are to be avoided. Stowage must, therefore, be easily acces-

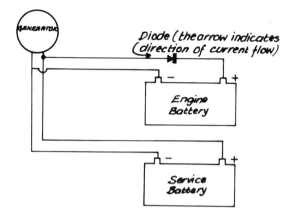

Fig 11.1 A blocking diode in the circuit to ensure that the service battery cannot drain the engine battery

sible and it is vital that lead/acid batteries can be topped up with distilled water without difficulty. Batteries are heavy and will have to be taken ashore when the boat is laid up. It should be possible, therefore, to lift them out without straining one's back or barking one's knuckles. The gases given off by batteries can produce an explosive mix and so good ventilation is a must. The air inlet should be at the bottom of the battery compartment with the outlet at the top. This means that care must be taken to ensure that rain and spray do not find their way down onto the batteries. If natural ventilation just cannot be provided, fans will be needed, and these must be fitted with flameproof motors to avoid the risk of fire. For the same reason, there should be no smoking or naked lights near the batteries, especially after charging when hydrogen is given off, and care should be exercised when handling wander leads etc which could cause a spark. It is unwise to fit any switches or fuses near the batteries as these, too, can cause sparking. Last, but by no means least, batteries must be properly secured. They should be mounted in a suitable drip tray – GRP, steel (alkaline only) or lead (acid only) – in such a way that they will not come adrift even if the boat were to roll right over. All connections should receive regular attention; taken apart, cleaned, dried and retightened and then coated with a smear of petroleum jelly.

Most of us have to accept the charging unit fitted to our auxiliary engine, be it a dynamo or an alternator. However, we may find that this is just not man enough to keep both the engine-starting and service batteries properly charged. If we use the auxiliary for a reasonable but insufficient period each day, we can consider adding a further generator and driving it by vee-belts from some convenient part of the engine. In such cases it is well worth looking at an alternator rather than a dynamo. Apart from the fact that alternators produce more power weight for weight than dynamos they can be run far faster. This means that they can be geared to give a reasonable charge at quite low engine revolutions without the risk of damage as the speed is increased. They are still more expensive than dynamos but, thanks to the increasing numbers now fitted to cars, the differential is closing. A different type of charging circuit will be required and a suitable system is shown in Fig 11.2. The alternative is to use the existing unit for the engine battery only and the additional one for the service battery. In this case there should be a way of changing the leads so that both units can feed either battery in an emergency such as a dynamo failure.

If such a system can be made to work, it is probably preferable to installing a standby generator set. However, consider the second rule which states: 'electrical power *must* be available from some source which does not require electrical power for starting purposes.' In other words, if your auxiliary can be started only with the electric starter, you must carry a standby generator with an engine that can be started by hand. If this rule is broken not only may you find yourself without power at a critical moment but you may also have no navigation lights when it matters most – in a busy sea lane.

The small, portable generating set has improved greatly in recent years and can provide both 12v DC for battery charging and 240v AC which is a great benefit at fitting-out times and for general repairs and maintenance as one can then use normal power tools. If, however, 240v AC will not be needed, it is wiser to avoid generators which provide this facility as it is an obvious danger, especially to small children – a danger which can be completely avoided.

A second factor to consider is the fuel. Whilst most small units are powered by two-stroke engines calling for a petrol/oil mix, four-stroke units accepting neat petrol and others with conversions to propane are also available. There is much to be said for a properly installed generator, piped into the craft's gas supply, fitted with an

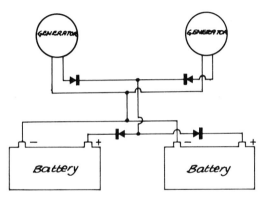

Fig 11.2 Using blocking diodes when two generators are used to charge two batteries

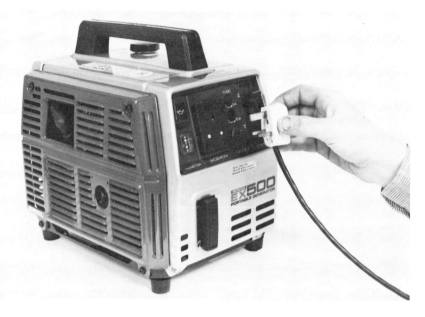

Plate 11.1 A small portable generator. This Honda model offers both 240V AC and 12V DC

Plate 11.2 The RO-TOW-VANE unit is fitted near the stern and operates both as a wind vane and, when suitable speeds are reached, is water operated by towing a line ending in an impeller similar to those used to operate mechanical logs

extension exhaust system taking all the gases safely over the side and mounted in a sound-proofed box to reduce the noise level. The advantages include completely removing the risk of fuel spilling everywhere when refilling the tank – easily done, especially at sea – and reducing the risk of dirt in the fuel line or carburettor. The disadvantages are that such an installation is inevitably more expensive than a fully portable unit and one loses this portability. If the generator is not going to be used away from the boat this latter point will not matter.

At all times the exhaust gases must go well clear as they are both hot and poisonous. In port this presents little difficulty as they can be run on deck (but to the annoyance of all others in the vicinity) but at sea, just when it may be needed very badly, there can be a problem. If it cannot be solved simply then a permanent installation should be considered.

The use of the natural forces of wind, solar and water power is enjoying a vogue and they may be harnessed to give us some of the power we need. The problem is that few single items of equipment will generate all our requirements. None of the manufacturers of solar power equipment give helpful figures and one is forced to conclude that few cruising men would consider such an installation. Wind power, on the other hand, is worth thinking about as there are some very good units now available. Depending on the size one can expect outputs of between ½ to 5 amps giving an average daily input in the order of 150 to 1200 watt hours – if the wind is reasonably co-operative. From these figures one could deduce that a suitably sized unit would answer all our needs but, unfortunately, the wind may well choose the two weeks of our cruise to fall below the required speeds. There is no doubt that a small unit, which can be left to its own devices when we are away from the boat, is a great blessing as it means we shall have fully charged batteries whenever we return. There is also no doubt that a larger unit is beneficial if we can afford to back it up with an engine-driven generator for use when the wind fails but few can afford such luxuries. Water power can be harnessed when we are sailing and Balance Engineering manufacture a unit (called a Ro-Tow-Vane) which can be driven by a trailing rotor or by its wind vane.

Lighting

We can use electricity, gas or paraffin and all are perfectly acceptable.

Electricity has the superb advantage that it is available at the flick of a switch. However, we have already seen that the demand can be quite high. Tungsten lamps are still the most commonly fitted even though fluorescent tubes consume less power. This is probably due partly to the higher initial cost and partly to the problems of radio interference. Most modern fluorescent units are fitted with adequate suppressors and should not create problems. Even if some other form of lighting is used, there is a strong case for fitting one or two electric lights (simple tungsten are best in this case) so that they can be used when arriving on board in the dark while the other lights are lit or in an emergency at sea.

Gas provides a very bright, white light. A fairly complex piped installation is required and, since every joint is a potential weakness, such an installation should be backed up with a 'sniffer' or gas-leak detector. There is, of course, no need to refill gas lamps and they are clean. Personally I do not like the quality of light they provide, it is far too cold for my taste, and I find the noise annoying.

Paraffin, on the other hand, is smelly and messy. The Tilley type of lamp with a mantle produces a similar type of light to the gas light – and makes the same noise. Many people swear by them but I prefer the warmer light which comes from wick lamps. Since these produce less light, they must be positioned carefully if one is to be able to read by them without discomfort.

The main problems when using paraffin are the need to refill the

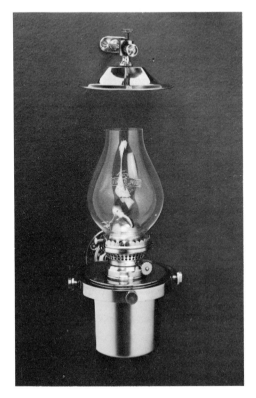

Plate 11.3 A simple but very effective form of lighting is this neat gimballed paraffin lamp (*South Western Marine Factors*)

lamps – probably daily – and the need to keep the wicks trimmed and the chimneys clean. About half the available light can be lost if this routine maintenance is ignored. Filling can be made far easier if one uses something like an old metal teapot for the job rather than a funnel; it is far simpler to see when the lamp base is full that way. Cleaning chimneys which are coated with the usual brown deposit is no problem. The best tool is a piece of paper kitchen towel as it seems to combine the right qualities of roughness and absorbency. This should be damped with a little paraffin, the glass cleaned and then polished using a dry bit of the towel. If the lamp has been turned up too high and the chimney is coated with a black soot the problem is rather different. This soot is filthy and oily and the temptation to wash the chimney in a bowl with hot water and detergent should be avoided as it takes twice as long to clean the bowl out afterwards as it does to clean the glass. Again, paper kitchen towels are used. Start by using a dry towel to remove the worst and then follow the above technique although a new towel will be needed to polish the chimney afterwards.

Both gas and paraffin lights produce a fair amount of heat and many who use them find that no other heat source is required. Our technique when the weather is not too cold is to light the lamps first thing, even when it is not dark, and also the gas oven. Once the boat is at a reasonable temperature these are switched off. Usually no further heat is needed until it becomes dark and the lamps are lit again.

Heating

The best form of heating is a solid-fuel stove as this creates no condensation, provides a source of air movement (and thus ventilation), does not create any toxic fumes and helps to get rid of rubbish. However, few small cruising boats are large enough to take such a stove although it is well worth making efforts to fit one in if cruising will include the colder months of the year.

Obviously, care has to be taken when installing any fire in a boat but there is no reason why there should be any greater fire risk than there is with a fire at home. Some stoves, such as the Tortoise and certain wood-burning stoves, become hot. A good air gap must be left around these as insulating woodwork with asbestos sheet is not a good idea. It is quite possible for the wood to be charring away out of sight behind the insulation.

The same applies to metal chimneys which are best protected by fitting a cylinder of perforated or expanded metal around them with a gap of at least 7.5cm (3in). A metal chimney is best as it enables one to rig up a drying cupboard around it which is a great boon. Beware of using galvanised iron for this as the fumes from the fire will soon start to corrode it. The problem with metal chimneys is that they tend to draw badly until they are hot whereas asbestos draws much better, but it also wastes a lot of the heat.

Where the chimney passes through the deck is always a danger point and the chimney must be properly insulated. Some fittings rely on a trough which is filled with water to cool it. If the fire is to be used at sea this type should be avoided as the motion usually throws the water out and the whole thing becomes far too hot.

The chimney above the deck should be easily removable and the stub fitted with a cap. Some people use a screwed fitting but a tight-fitting cap that fits over (not into) the stub has always worked well. There may be a problem caused by the down draught from the sails. Fitting a cowl may prove to be the answer but often fails to provide a complete cure. A short length of pipe with a 45 degree bend which fits easily enough to be rotated as required, but tight enough to stay put after it has been adjusted, is simple and usually works.

It may be that we just cannot fit a solid-fuel stove and must look at other heating methods. This means that we will almost certainly have to accept one of three other difficulties – condensation, problems in obtaining fuel or a high electrical demand.

Gas heaters are available which convert the fuel into heat without a flame using the catalytic process. These may be obtained in various shapes and sizes including quite small bulkhead units. Heat outputs are high for the size of the heater and the appliances are safe to use provided they are properly installed although any boat fitted with them should be equipped with a 'sniffer'. The problem is that they create water vapour which means condensation.

Paraffin stoves, provided they are screwed to the deck or to a bulkhead, are also safe. They must, of course, be filled and the wicks need to be kept properly trimmed but we have used them when there have been children and dogs on board without problems – except for condensation. It is said that a paraffin stove produces a pint of condensation for every pint of fuel burnt and I am prepared to believe it is true.

Both the above heaters – gas and paraffin – take the oxygen required from the air in the cabin and, since they do not produce a partial vacuum like a stove with a flue, do not encourage ventilation. It is quite possible for the oxygen level to drop dangerously low. I have sat in our saloon and watched the oil lamps, which I had filled only a few hours before, burn lower and lower. Stupidly I have blown them out to refill them, only to realise as I opened the hatch to get the fuel that the problem was a lack of oxygen. After a few frights such as this, we settled down to find the right way to use the combination of paraffin heating and lighting.

The only way is to provide rather more heat than is really required and to create ample ventilation. This draws in sufficient oxygen and takes out a lot of the water vapour before it has time to condense. Where we had two stoves fitted, we installed three – each with a suitable vent located above it (or nearly so). It sounds silly to throw away heat and add 50 per cent to the fuel bill but boats are not very large and so it is 50 per cent of not very much – and it works. I suspect that the same method would work with gas heaters as well.

A number of firms sell heaters which use a special liquid fuel which they claim produces little or no water vapour. The problem is that fuel sources are few and far apart and so I have never fitted one although I have been tempted on a number of occasions. A friend of mine uses one and is very pleased with it but his mooring is very close to one of the chandlers who stock the fuel.

Hot-air systems are superb. The heater itself draws air from outside, heats it by passing it through a heat exchanger and blows it through ducts to outlets in the cabins. Usually situated under a cockpit locker, it uses a separate air inlet for the burner and the waste gases are piped away, usually to an outlet near the stern. The ideal situation is achieved – no condensation and plenty of ventilation plus the possibility of rigging up a drying cabinet and even using an outlet with a wandering duct as a hair dryer. Such heaters burn a variety of fuels, diesel making most sense if this is used for the auxiliary and worth thinking about if not. However, as always, there is a price to pay – in this case the electrical demand of the fan motor used to blow the air through the ducting. A reasonable figure would be about 40 watts – which adds up to nearly 1,000 watt hours per day if the heater is run continuously. Given a motor-sailer which is generating ample power, this type must be the first choice.

Incidentally, before leaving the question of heating, I would like to mention an experiment I carried out during the pretty miserable summer of 1981. On the principle that black absorbs heat and white reflects it we painted the hull black – the interior was already white. It seemed to work; the hull absorbed quite a lot of heat even with only very modest sunshine. We waited for the problems we had been warned about, such as paint blistering and planks shrinking, but we waited in vain. I suspect that it would take more than the usual British summer to create these difficulties. The black certainly showed salt stains and so on and we found we were washing it down rather more frequently but this seemed to be a small price to pay. During the few very hot days we experienced, it certainly became very warm below but it was never uncomfortable as we increased the ventilation by adding a couple of opening portholes and modified the forehatch.

Cookers and Cooking

Good, hot food is one of the keys to successful cruising. It follows that the easier and more comfortable the cook finds working in the galley the better. Galleys should be sited where the motion is at a minimum and light and ventilation at a maximum. It is helpful if, in addition, the cook can be in fairly easy contact with the rest of the crew as cooking can be a lonely business. In practice, this means that the galley should be just inside the companionway and aft of the saloon. The problems with such a layout are that the cook tends to block the companionway and the cooking smells are taken forward with the natural draught to fill the accommodation. Even so, this is the generally accepted position as other sites create other snags which are usually less acceptable.

There is a wide range of cookers available from simple single-burner pressurised paraffin stoves to full-sized domestic gas cookers running off bottled gas.

So long as pressurised paraffin stoves are kept clean and the correct lighting sequence is followed, there should not be any problem. The principle is the same in all cases. Paraffin is passed from a tank where it is kept under pressure up through pipes which lie in the flame where it is vaporised and then out through a jet above which it burns. Since the vapour cannot be created until these pipes are hot, they must be pre-heated in some way. This is achieved by filling a special trough beneath the pipes with methylated spirit, which is lit and allowed to burn away completely before the paraffin is pumped through. As the meths goes out, the air valve on the tank is closed and the pump is given a few strokes to provide the pressure. The paraffin should come out of the jet as a stream of white vapour which is lit using another match. If the paraffin comes out as a liquid, the air valve is opened to release the pressure and more meths is added to the trough to continue the pre-heating sequence. Pressure should never be applied until the meths has burnt away as, should the pipes be too cool to vaporise the paraffin, the resulting liquid stream will catch alight and flare up dangerously. A draught shield may be needed during this pre-heating but the stove will work quite well in a draught after it has been lit. Generally speaking, these stoves should be slung in gimbals as it is difficult to keep the meths in the trough if the stove is being thrown about. Packing the trough with an old lamp wick helps in this respect.

Stoves with two burners sharing a common pressurised tank are available. In this case the tank is kept pressurised except when it is being filled and each burner is controlled by a valve. As paraffin is safe to store and easy to find in most places, these stoves are ideal for the smaller boat. Older types 'roared' quite loudly but modern stoves can be bought which run almost silently and, although some people claim that the 'roarers' are more efficient in a draught, there is no real reason for purchasing the noisy units. Every now and then the jets become blocked, or partly so, and have to be 'pricked'. Modern stoves include a self-pricking device which makes this job easier. However, constant pricking soon wears the jets and they become enlarged. To reduce blocking to a minimum, the fuel should be stored in clean containers and passed through a funnel with a filter when filling the stove.

Although these stoves will take an oven which fits on top of the burners, there are no paraffin stoves with a grill – the only major disadvantage.

Pressurised alcohol (meths) stoves work on a similar principle to the above although they require less pre-heating as meths is more volatile than paraffin. Such stoves can be obtained with up to three burners and an oven but, again, grills cannot be fitted. Not all alcohol stoves use pressure. Very simple, and safe, to use is the type where the burners sit on top of a tank which is filled with an absorbent material which feeds the fuel up to a wick where it vaporises. Less smelly than paraffin, meths is more expensive. The choice between the two is largely a matter of personal preference.

Bottled gas has become increasingly popular and stoves with grills and ovens are readily available. The range is enormous from simple single-burner stoves mounted directly onto a small cylinder of gas, to full-sized domestic cookers modified to accept either butane or propane. From the cooking point of view, these are ideal. They can be slung in gimbals and fitted with fiddles to hold pots and pans in position and are as easy to light and control as any other gas cooker.

However, gas is a dangerous bedfellow and great care must be taken if it is to be used on board. It is heavier than air and so sinks to the bilges where it can form a highly explosive mixture with air, ready and willing to ignite given a spark or naked light. The cylinders must be stored in a separate compartment (or on deck) so that any leakage drains over the side. All piping should be installed by a person who thoroughly understands the problem and it is extremely sensible to fit a 'sniffer' which can detect any gas in the bilges and sound an alarm. The main valve on the cylinder should be turned off whenever there is no need for gas and no appliance should be switched on until there is a lighted match in position. This is by no means alarmist. There have been many cases of fires on board through gas leaking and not a few fine craft have been totally destroyed. Frankly, gas is best left ashore but if it is to be used all precautions must be taken to ensure safety.

We have already noted that solid-fuel stoves for heating are first class. On larger vessels it is possible to combine this with the cooking requirements and install a Rayburn or other solid-fuel cooking stove.

These are, of course, both large and heavy, therefore few cruising boats can be equipped with them. The only disadvantage is that they cannot be slung in gimbals but, since they are usually found only on large craft, this is something one learns to live with.

Before leaving the question of cookers it is worth noting that all cookers slung in gimbals should be fitted with a locking device to hold them upright when in port. This avoids the risk of the cooker being knocked (especially by a child) at a time when there may be no fiddles fitted and a hot pan falling off.

Cooking at sea is very little different from cooking at home, provided that the cook is feeling up to the job. There is no reason why the cook should be any more immune from seasickness than any other member of the crew and being stuck below surrounded by the smells of cooking is no place for a person with a queasy stomach. However, hot food is a must if crew efficiency is not to suffer. A pressure cooker can solve the problem if those aboard enjoy eating stews. A meal can be prepared and cooked in port, the pressure cooker being allowed to cool with the weights left in position. It will keep quite happily for quite some time like that and all the cook then need do is to heat it up before serving. Pies and pasties which only require heating are also worth considering. After a few days, tummies will have settled down and one can revert to a normal menu.

Food storage, on the other hand, presents certain special problems. Few cruising boats are fitted with refrigerators and a cool larder of some sort has to suffice. In the old days these were often to be found on deck where the sun overheated them during the day. It is better to choose some spot below the waterline and against the skin of the boat, such as a deep cockpit locker, where sufficient ventilation can be provided. Air vents should be provided top and bottom, covered with metal gauze to keep out unwanted insects, while positioning the larder against the outside of the hull helps to keep it cool. Care should be taken to ensure that there is no risk of tainting the food by proximity to fuel, especially diesel, and if this cannot be achieved in the cockpit some other site will have to be found.

Under normal circumstances when cruising around the coast, particularly with children who want a run ashore fairly frequently, fresh food can be used most of the time as it will not have to keep for more than two or three days. However, it is important to carry other stores to meet contingencies, and the choice must be between dried and tinned foods.

Dried foods can be stored in old ice-cream containers and it is usually a fairly simple job to make a rack to take these. It is a mistake to have them all the same size as one does not carry large quantities of, say, tea but would not wish to store it with any other foodstuff as there is always a risk of cross-contamination of the flavours. However, large, half-filled containers waste a great deal of space. We use such containers to carry all dried foods including sugar, tea, coffee, rice, porridge, etc as well as dried soups and vegetables. Worth special mention is dried milk. This is not only cheaper than fresh milk but can be made up in small quantities so removing the risk of it going off. Incidentally, some dried foods are just not obtainable in the ordinary retail shops and some which are may be inferior to those available to the catering trade. We have found, for example, that the dried milk packaged for the catering trade is far easier to mix than that usually on the shop shelves. Some catering cash and carry stores are willing to allow one to stock up for a cruise but if there is not one in your area it is worth befriending an hotelier or restaurateur and ordering through him. Apart from anything else, he will probably be able to give you good advice.

Some foods are not available in dried form and one must look at tins. Meat products, carrots and some puddings are the only tinned foods we carry but there are many others, especially fruits, which are invaluable if there are small children aboard. The favoured place for storing tins is in the bilge but precautions have to be taken. Paper labels must be removed – if they are left in situ they will soon come adrift if there is any water below and then they will almost certainly block the bilge pumps. It is a grave mistake to rely on memory as to contents and all tins should be marked using a broad felt-tip pen. If they are to be stored for any length of time, a quick coat of varnish retards rusting.

Although dried foods take less space and are lighter than their tinned equivalents, they all require more water when cooking. This may mean that additional water storage will be required, but I consider water easier to store and carry than most foodstuffs and so do not consider this a grave disadvantage.

Water Storage and Water Systems

The simplest form of water storage is a plastic can from which it is poured when required. It is almost certainly worth arranging a supply piped to the sink unless the boat is very small and relies on a washing-up bowl which is emptied over the side. Incidentally, if this is the case, the largest water container should be 11 litre (2½ gal) as anything bigger is impossible to handle easily and even this size is getting near the limit. The washing-up bowl should have straight sides to reduce the risk of water slopping out of it.

It is a mistake to try and fit a header tank which gravity feeds to taps at the sink. Apart from the fact that water is heavy and should not be stored at high level, this is asking for waste. Not only will people just use too much but a leaking or dripping tap can consume surprising amounts of precious water – water you may have had to carry for some distance. Far better is to install a pump. This may be electrically operated but we have already discussed the problems of creating additional electrical demand and these, too, tend to encourage wasteful use of water. Better is either a hand- or foot-operated pump, the latter being best as it means both hands are free when it is being operated.

Incidentally, if electrical pumps are used, it is possible to create running hot water using a gas water heater. Although these are quite efficient they do, of course, increase electrical demand as higher water pressures are required to pump through the heater than are needed to just feed a sink.

Water tanks may be rigid, manufactured from galvanised iron, or flexible, usually made from neoprene although a number of other plastics are also used. Rigid tanks are to be preferred even though this means one has the choice of wasting valuable space or having them made to order. The tanks should be as near to the midships as possible so as not to affect the fore and aft trim regardless of how full they are. Although copper piping used to be fitted, plastic piping has the advantage that it does not cause any electrolytic action. All rigid tanks should be fitted with large manhole covers so that they can be cleaned out and inspected as required. If flexible tanks are fitted, care must be taken to guard against chafe. It is surprising how quickly a partially filled tank wears as it moves backwards and forwards against some projection such as a stringer. The easiest way of avoiding this is probably to rig up slats for the tank to lie in.

If more than one tank is used, each will be piped to a manifold from which a further pipe will run to each pump on the freshwater circuit. There should be a valve fitted in each of the pipes from the tanks so that it can be isolated. One tank should be kept isolated so as to create a reserve but the reserve tank should be the first one used after refilling to avoid carrying stale water. All rigid tanks should be fitted with air vents in the form of pipes running up to just under the deck head where they should be turned back to face downwards to stop dirt getting in. Flexible tanks do not need vents as they collapse when the water is taken out. Although it is usual to use a separate pipe for filling, a single filling pipe to the manifold is perfectly satis-factory (remember to open the valves of the tanks to be filled, it is annoying to find one was forgotten). If the filling point is higher than the top of the vent pipes, it is possible to cause flooding. All the pumps we have had have allowed water to flow through and so water flowing out into the sink has acted as 'level gauge', but there may be models which do not behave like this so it might be worth checking first to find out.

Before leaving water altogether, it is worth looking at the use of

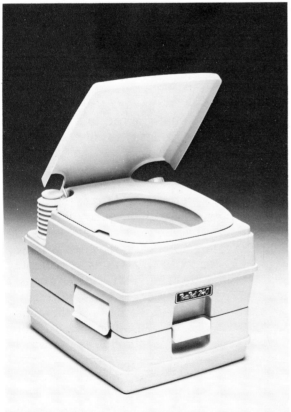

Plate 11.4 Probably the simplest sea toilet available, the Lavac Zenith by Blake & Sons is installed with a separate pump fitted in the outlet pipe which runs from the lower connection. This may be either manually or electrically operated. With the lid closed this pump both cleans effluent and, by forming a vacuum, draws in flushing water. If inlet and outlet hoses are looped up above water-line, sea cocks may be left open with no risk of flooding (they should still be closed in heavy weather)

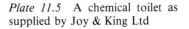

Plate 11.5 A chemical toilet as supplied by Joy & King Ltd

sea water. This is perfectly satisfactory for dishwashing if a detergent is used and can be used for clothes so long as the final rinsing is carried out in fresh water. Unfortunately, some river and estuary water is filthy and cannot be used at all. Even so, it is worth rigging up a second pump over the sink for sea water – fitting a sea cock that can be turned off if required.

Unfortunately, water has to be brought aboard. In some places a hose can be used which is ideal. The inside of the hose will soon become covered in green and brown algae if no precautions are taken. However, this can be kept to a minimum if corks are fitted to both ends to keep out the air when the hose is not in use. In some places, the only method is to carry the water aboard in plastic containers. Although a man can carry two 23 litre (5 gal) containers, it is probably best to standardise on 11 litre (2½ gal) ones which can be carried by other members of the crew. At sea these should be kept sufficiently full to be useful but not full enough to sink. This means that they can be attached to the inflatable or liferaft by lines so that, should one have to abandon ship, one is assured of a water supply. One often hears of folk who have thrown full water containers over the side – only to watch them sink out of sight.

Toilets

The simplest comfortable toilet for use at sea is a bucket under a wooden seat. There is absolutely nothing wrong with this system as sea water is a mild disinfectant and it is easy to keep the bucket perfectly clean. It has the advantage that, unlike a standard sea toilet, there is no call to drill holes through the hull. However, most boats are fitted with a standard sea toilet which has two pumps fitted – one to pump in fresh sea water, the other to pump out. These toilets need occasional maintenance if they are to work well but this maintenance is often neglected and the pumps work badly. Both the inlet and outlet should, of course, be fitted with sea cocks which should be kept closed when the toilet is not in use.

It is, in my view, very antisocial to use either of the above in a harbour – our inshore waters are quite filthy enough as it is. Fortunately it is not necessary as there are portable toilets on the market which store the effluent until it can be disposed of either out at sea or down a public toilet. There are two types available, fixed tank and separate tank. With the latter models, the holding tank can be removed from the unit so that it can be carried away for emptying. This is far easier than lumping the whole toilet and is worth the extra cost. Frankly, if there is only room for one toilet I would choose one of these. Apart from the environmental considerations they are just as pleasant to use as a standard sea toilet, if not more so.

12
The Crew

So far we have considered some of the more basic aspects of seamanship and navigation and looked at some of the items of equipment needed to achieve a successful cruise. However, cruising is not just about boats, equipment, tides and seamanship, it is about people – people on holiday, people enjoying themselves, people sharing moments of magical calm and moments of boisterous uncertainty.

We may spend months planning and preparing for the perfect cruise and, at the end of our cruise, the deck log may well record that we have executed our plans with precision. This is how it should be but rarely happens because the deck log is the least important record we have on board although it is no less vital for that. It is the personal logs of the members of the crew that tell of the true success or failure of the cruise for if all on board have failed to enjoy themselves then the cruise has been a failure regardless of contrary evidence from the deck log. For this reason it often happens that the original plan has to be altered and, indeed, one prime cause of failure, in human terms, is the belief that the cruise plan must be adhered to come what may.

First of all, then, we must look at the crew and consider what sort of cruising is most suited to them. This can be a difficult problem for my idea of the perfect cruise may not suit you at all as yours may not suit me – we all look for different things from our cruising. This applies just as much to crews. The experienced day sailor may look forward to extended passages and evenings spent in the social atmosphere of a club bar but there can be nothing more boring for young children who want to explore both ashore and, using the dinghy, the creeks and backwaters.

Let us consider the case of a fairly typical family of four. I hope that I will not be accused of being a male chauvinist in choosing such a crew, but it enables me to illustrate certain points. Father has considerable experience in both dinghies and day-sailers and has crewed in a few cruising boats; mother has limited experience although she has been out in the dinghy a few times; the two children aged ten and eight have no experience whatsoever.

The first thing to notice is that father is going to have to combine the roles of skipper, father and tutor. This will place considerable demands upon him for teaching, if it is done well, requires a great deal of dedication and patience. It also means that he will be carrying a heavy responsibility for, when things go wrong, as they will, and he starts to blame everyone else, as happens, he should stop a moment and consider that either he is failing as a skipper and is giving orders badly or he has failed as an instructor and the crew do not understand him or he has failed as a father and the crew do not wish to understand him. In short, he must learn as have all before him that the skipper takes the ultimate responsibility for every single thing that happens. In some ways his lot is more difficult than those in command of commercial craft for at least they do not have to worry about the crew's happiness as well as everything else. So, before planning any aspect of the cruise, father has to look at himself. Is he capable of handling the boat safely in all conditions? If the answer is 'no', then he must plan the cruise around his own limitations. If there are young children on board it is vital that the parents show them placid confidence at all times – it is not the time to stretch one's abilities and risk thoroughly frightening everyone. Next he must ask himself if he has the ability to be a good teacher. We all know how hard it is for a husband to teach a wife to drive a car – our typical father may well be planning to teach all his crew on their first cruise, a far harder task. Frankly, unless he feels that he can do the job properly, the best advice is to send the children to a sailing school to learn the rudiments. More children are put off sailing by their parents shouting at them than by any other means.

Cruising must combine both seamanship in its fullest sense with the ability to live on board in harmony – two separate subjects. We decided to tackle them separately and so we turned our backs on the sea for our first cruise and hired a narrow boat on an inland waterway. Far from worries of tides and navigational problems, we were able to find our feet among lush meadows and woodlands. Neither my wife nor her son – for we married when he was nearly ten – had any real experience, and this environment proved to be the perfect nursery school.

Soon they were learning to handle warps and even the boat as we worked through locks, gaining confidence as they learnt. They began to understand the need to work as a team – that there are moments when all one's attention must be on the boat, that orders have to be obeyed quickly and that there is a great sense of achievement in being part of a team which is working as a single unit. They began to see the benefits of planning and training so that the most complex evolutions could be carried out with the minimum of orders and fuss. These basic lessons stood us all in great stead later on.

More important, we learnt to live together in the fairly cramped quarters the boat offered. Granted we were in a stable boat which did not spend its time heeling at an angle of 30° but it was a good start.

I learnt a lot, too. At first I tended to do everything myself until I realised that this would soon lead to a bored and uninterested crew. In the end we all stood 'watches' at the helm and, whilst I stood by at first in case things went badly wrong, I tried very hard to let them make their own mistakes and so learn from them. This is surprisingly difficult, especially when there are other people looking on and one begins to feel embarrassed, but I am sure it is the right thing to do. It is far easier to snatch a rope away with a gruff 'Here, give that to me' than it is to watch a small boy making a complete hash of tying a bowline. It is also the quickest way to destroy his confidence and ensure that his next attempt will be even less successful.

It would be wrong to say that we learnt a great deal on that first cruise as far as boat handling is concerned. The most important thing was that we learnt how to tackle the whole subject. We learnt, if you like, how to learn. The crew learnt to trust my orders; I learnt to give them only after I had explained exactly what was required and why. We also learnt that cruising can be a peaceful, almost soporific, activity interlaced with moments of extreme activity. It is this combination that gives the cruising man so much pleasure – the sense of achievement of a task done well and the time to enjoy it. Inland waterways offer the perfect environment for this combination as the locks provide the necessary challenge – if you don't believe that, try working a fairly unhandy narrow boat into a lock beside a fully flowing weir with a smart cross wind blowing for good measure – and the quiet stretches between provide the contrast.

If you are thinking of cruising with a novice crew, a week or two spent on such a boat is well worth considering.

As far as the actual living is concerned, it must be remembered that we are talking about being on holiday and it is no holiday if the distaff side of the family does no more than to exchange one sink and one cooker for another, especially when the exchange is from a kitchen to a galley. Now is the time for a bit of role reversal, with the skipper actually doing some of the cooking. Whenever possible, whoever prepares the meal and cooks it should not clear away afterwards. The novice wife who is expected to do all the domestic work can hardly be blamed if, next year, she opts for the comfort of an hotel. Furthermore, there will come a time when the skipper will need to be freed of the helm to carry out some task that is beyond the physical capacity of any other member of the crew. It will be then that he is more than happy to be able to entrust it to his wife – so long as she has sufficient experience to be able to handle the boat as well as he can – experience that will not be gained cooped up below dealing with the greasy breakfast dishes.

The children, too, can help. At the very least they should be made responsible for looking after their own things, stowing them away when they have finished with them and generally keeping their own quarters tidy.

When under way, children can become incredibly bored in a surprisingly short period of time. Then they begin to fidget and get under foot. At sea they may well be frightened, especially if you have not explained to them what to expect and why certain things are happening – things like the home suddenly taking a list as you turn towards the wind. Shouting at them will only make matters worse and undermine their confidence. Careful and cheerful explanation of what is happening, quiet instruction in some task and then allocating them to that task will soon remove the trouble and, before long, will turn them into useful and responsible members of the crew. We will take a look at some suitable tasks later on.

The next stage will probably be in your own boat. There is a great deal to be said for making the first boat one that can be trailed and brought home during the winter. This offers two advantages. In the first place it enables you to cruise in areas which are most suited to you and your crew without the problems of finding somewhere where you can moor the boat – an increasingly difficult task as harbours become more and more popular and available spaces few and far between. Unfortunately it is often those areas best suited to novices in the cruising scene that have the longest waiting lists for moorings. The second advantage is that the family can get used to the boat at home when you cannot be out sailing. By the time the trailer is hitched to the car, the stores have been packed and excitement heightens in anticipation of 'the first cruise', all should know the name of every part on board as well as its function. Many small boats which can be towed easily are not really suitable for long offshore passages but this should not matter at this stage. It is unlikely that the crew will be ready for such voyaging nor will they yet know what sort of cruising really suits them and, since that will be a large factor in determining the best boat to buy, it is extremely unlikely that the first boat will be the last (unless, of course, it turns out that the first cruise is the last).

The alternative is to charter. This is a fine way to try out various areas and various types of boat. Unfortunately it does restrict the possibility of learning about the boat before the cruise, a disadvantage which – to my way of thinking – makes charter more suitable for the more experienced who wish to cruise in boats which are far too expensive for ownership to be considered.

The best area to choose for the first cruise in tidal waters will include expanses of inland, or at least sheltered, waters, so that there is somewhere for the younger members of the crew to learn to handle the dinghy and so that one can continue sailing even if the weather turns out to be less kind than had been hoped.

There are four obvious choices, all in the southern part of the country which is a pity. These are the Falmouth area with its wide expanses of well-sheltered water and interesting, if short, cruises to other parts; Poole harbour where Baden-Powell used to camp with his boys on Brownsea Island; the Harwich area with its rivers; and Plymouth, a very central point from which to plan a number of short cruises as there are good harbours both to east and west. The Solent is probably too busy for a first cruise, although many would add it to the list.

The first two or three days should be set aside for training. This sounds very boring but pays massive dividends in the long run. Naturally, the exact programme will depend on the conditions as well as the skills of the various members of the crew, but a typical three-day training scheme might well be as follows.

Training

Of necessity, we will have to launch our boat if we have trailed it and this means, in all probability, taking it to a suitable anchorage. If possible, find a nice quiet spot where you can try out some of the various training activities without too many curious eyes watching and putting everyone off. For this reason, I suggest an anchorage rather than a mooring. In any event, it is easier to anchor than to moor when single-handed and, for this trip, the skipper will be almost in the same position.

Our first training activity will, therefore, be anchoring under power. Explain to the crew that it is essential that the anchor cable is not dropped on top of the anchor and so we need to know how the boat will behave when power is taken off and she is allowed to drift. In a small boat the engine is probably an outboard with no reverse, and so this lesson is very important. Try cutting the engine as the boat faces into the tide, into the wind, across both and so on, and watch to see how she performs. If you keep up an interesting and entertaining commentary while carrying out these tests, it should be possible to keep the crew interested and avoid boredom. Explain to them that it is just as important for them to be able to judge what will happen as it will be their turn one day. Ask them what they think is likely to happen under certain circumstances and then try it out. An hour spent in this fashion will prove invaluable. Having satisfied yourself that you will be able to judge matters properly, choose a nice quiet stretch and hand over the helm for a few minutes while you go forward and flake the required cable out on deck. Return to the cockpit, take the way off the boat and back onto the foredeck to drop the anchor. So far, so good. Before this first training sessions ends, there are two jobs to do and you might as well start off doing things the right way. Now introduce the pelorus or the hand-bearing compass and show the crew how to take cross bearings so that you can check that the anchor is holding. Lastly, check the depth using the echo sounder or the lead, show the crew how you calculate the maximum depth at high water and then take them forward to see the depth markings on the cable as you veer the required amount and make all fast.

That is quite enough for the moment and so it's down below to make a well-earned cup and have a rest.

After this, if the wind and the tide are co-operating and you are lying head to the wind, it is time to start learning how to hoist and lower the sails. Each sail should be hoisted and lowered in turn by various combinations of the crew as this will soon determine who has the strength to do what. It is often possible for two young boys to handle the hoisting of the mainsail all on their own so long as there is a tackle fitted so that they can haul down on the boom after the sail is up – a small addition that can put another job within their grasp and therefore well worth fitting.

Although we are at anchor and, we hope, the sun is shining down on a calm day, now is the time to introduce the rules regarding wearing of safety harnesses. The best rule is to allow no one out of the cockpit without a safety harness at any time. It is a bore, but one cannot expect children to abide by the rule unless the adults set a good example.

Personally, I like to see children free of the parent ship as soon as possible so I would now turn to boat drill in the dinghy. It may be, and often is, that the children can already handle the dinghy and so the next 'training session' can be turned into fun. In any event, all should wear lifejackets when in the dinghy. If the children can already row, they can be sent off to explore – but give them a particular objective. This could be to go to a beach marked on the chart to see if it is suitable for bathing, or to row to the head of a creek and find out if there is a shop there. In any event, they should be told to stay within sight and the direction should be chosen so that their trip is 'fail safe'. By this I mean that if, for example, they were to lose an oar, the prevailing conditions would take them to safety. This trip should not be made with an ebb tide and with the wind blowing them towards the harbour entrance. If there is any doubt about the conditions, it is better to make two trips, both with an adult.

That will probably be more than enough for the first day in view of the fact that it will have included driving down, launching and so on.

As 'man overboard' is the most usual form of emergency, the first training session next day should be devoted to dealing with it when under power. A lifebelt or something similar can be used as the 'man', and it can be thrown overboard while on various courses. Take it in turns to decide who has gone over the side and make that person sit out of the way and keep quiet. The youngest remaining member of the crew can be given the job of keeping watch on the 'body'. The aim is for the crew to be able to cope satisfactorily when the victim is the skipper himself. If the weather is reasonable and the water not too cold, it is helpful if this training session can include practice in getting the body back on board. The 'body' should wear a lifejacket and give the minimum of assistance to the rest of the crew. Apart from teaching people to have confidence in their lifejackets, this will highlight any problems and give you the chance to sort them out. Are you sure that your wife and children could pull you back on board when you are too exhausted or hurt to be able to help them? You should be.

Now for a bit of sailing. Obviously stage one is to tack, gybe and carry on tacking and gybing until all know what to do. Again, try it with various crew members carrying out different tasks. If any over-night or long passages are planned, it is probable that watches will be split between the skipper and the youngest child in one watch with the mate and the eldest child in the other. Try out the evolutions with each watch 'off duty' in turn.

As children soon become bored, an early lunch in some spot where they can fish or go ashore in the dinghy is not a bad idea. In any event, most skippers will find these training sessions pretty exhaust-ing and it is vital that tempers are not lost or harsh words used. Training children to enjoy sailing requires as much tact and patience as training a young horse.

There should be two aims for the afternoon session; to repeat the man overboard drill under sail and to practise picking up a mooring buoy under both sail and power. By this time, the children should be quite capable of taking the helm as well as both the adults, and there is no good reason why the skipper should not let the others have as much time at it as possible. There is the temptation to take the tiller when things look as though they might go wrong – avoid it like the plague, there is no quicker way than this to destroy the novice's confi-dence which should be building up nicely by this time.

The third day dawns and one of the needs will be fresh stores. That fits in very well with the morning plan – to practise going alongside a quay or jetty. It may be, of course, that this is not possible and one will have to use the dinghy instead. However, if there is a suitable place, you can take a leaf out of the aeroplane pilot's book and try some 'circuits and bumps'. This means going round and round, bringing up against the quay until attached by a boathook, and then casting off and trying again. If the children have learnt quickly it is possible that they could try this once each; but the important thing is to achieve good team work and so the usual plan is for the skipper and youngest child to be in the cockpit, skipper at the helm and youngster handling the stern warps, whilst mate and eldest child are on the foredeck, one to handle the boathook and then fenders and the other to go ashore with the head rope.

The last part of the pre-cruise training is to reef the main and change jibs as required. Again this will be teamwork and how that team is organised will depend on the various skills that have been acquired in the earlier work. It is a good plan to work against a stopwatch (the second hand of an ordinary watch will do, we are not looking for great accuracy) so that there is some measure of performance. It is amazing how quickly the job can be done when this sort of competitive spirit is introduced, but it must never be forgotten that safety is more important than speed!

If I seem to have laboured this question of training it is because one sees so little carried out outside the world of the sailing schools. It is just as important for the modern cruising crew to be efficient as it was for the sailors in Nelson's navy, and they spent much of their time perfecting their skills. Some would argue that it is better to learn as you go along. I can't agree. We have already mentioned that husbands find it very difficult to teach their wives to drive a car. Many, many times I have heard parents screaming at their children and at each other when in boats; usually you will find that the one being yelled at hasn't a clue what has gone wrong. A reasonably comprehensive training session, carried out when the results don't really matter and in a calm atmosphere, is a far better approach but each period should be kept reasonably short and should be brought to an abrupt halt if the children tire or the skipper's temper begins to fray. Enough, let us get on and look at some of the other aspects of 'living on board'.

The Very Young

People have cruised with children of all ages and all has gone well. This says much for the planning and forethought of the parents as well as for their attitude.

Babies on board present few real problems. Naturally one has to be equipped to cope with them but the very young can sleep in a carrycot which has been well secured. The cabin sole is probably the best place for this although some people fix the carrycot onto a bunk. Feeding presents no difficulty as the quantities of food are small and most will be tinned. Disposable nappies are, of course, essential. The main problem is carrying a baby safely from boat to dinghy and from dinghy ashore, but a variety of body slings are available so that the baby can be carried on an adult's chest. These slings are often supplied with ties so that both hands can be free but the baby remains secure.

It would seem that few babies are worried by seasickness and they seem to delight in the boat's motion – perhaps it reminds them of earlier days – and so most of the difficulties are mechanical rather than psychological. Other items of equipment that could be useful include the canvas hammock chairs (the plastic ones are a bit hard and can give the baby a nasty bang if the boat is moving rather a lot), a playpen with net sides and a baby bouncer. All must be fitted properly, of course, but this is usually quite a simple matter.

As they grow older and can no longer sleep in a carrycot, the net-sided playpen can be used instead. The frame can be bolted down to a bunk from which the mattress has been removed and the net sides ensure that the baby will not be breathing stale air. If those available on the market cannot be fitted conveniently, a similar arrangement can be made fairly easily.

The real fun starts when the child begins to crawl. The first essential is to rig up netting around the guard rails, pulpit and pushpit so that they cannot fall overboard regardless of what happens. The next problem to tackle is the question of stowage generally and the galley in particular. Unlike at home where it is generally possible to put the various things to be kept out of the grasp of small hands higher and higher as the reach of the child increases, all such items have to be stowed away in lockers with child-proof catches. This can be a bit of a nuisance as many storage spaces will not be fitted with any door at all. However, it is worth while as it means one can relax even when the toddler is crawling around below without supervision.

The galley will be one danger point that will doubtless exercise the ingenuity of the skipper. If the layout of the accommodation lends itself to fitting some gate to keep the toddler well clear, this is probably the best answer. Unfortunately it is rarely possible. As the top of the cooker will be lower than the one at home, there is no point in pretending that a greater danger does not exist and some way must be found to stop the child from burning itself. I have seen a rather clever wire-mesh guard which could be pulled down and fitted to hooks; it was made out of link fencing and was held up quite simply with two short lanyards which were looped over hooks screwed into the deckhead. Obviously one does not intend to leave the cooker alight unless there is supervision, but it can be annoying to have to switch off the heat during cooking when help is required on deck – in fact, this is when risks are taken and an accident occurs.

Another irritating habit of the very young is to switch on some electrical device and so waste the valuable power from the battery. Either all switches should be contained in a central box with a suitable cover or there should be one master switch which is key-operated.

Under way small children must be contained safely below. Most parents tend to make the longer passages at night when the children are asleep, which is probably the best solution. Shorter day-time passages must however be taken into consideration and a playpen can be the answer. It should be possible to fit it securely inside the cabin so that the child can see the adult in the cockpit but not so that it blocks the companion way. Unless the boat is fitted with either a fixed table or a centreboard, this is usually no problem.

As soon as a child is capable of climbing over the netted guard rails the problems become rather different for now it cannot be allowed to crawl round the decks even when anchored or tied up alongside. Now is the time to start training with the safety belt. A jackstay must be rigged so that the child can be clipped on before leaving the cabin for the cockpit. The problems vary with each boat and with each child, but should not be exaggerated as they can be overcome with a bit of thought and care.

One danger sometimes overlooked is the risk of exposure. This is a double-edged sword involving both sun and cold. As far as cold is concerned, the greatest risks will be when in the dinghy. It is surprising how quickly a small child loses its body heat unless it is properly wrapped up. The sun can be a killer, too, and no baby should be put into the cockpit in the carrycot unless an awning is rigged to protect it.

As soon as the toddler becomes too large to carry in a sling, a folding pushchair and a very stout set of walking reins will be needed. If a lifejacket can be found small enough to support the child properly should it fall into the water, this can be added to the list. However, a badly fitting lifejacket is worse than useless: I once saw a child whose head was being kept firmly below the water by the collar of a lifejacket which was large enough to allow it to slip through; very prompt action saved the day but it is a lesson best learned second-hand. The reins should be used to secure the child in the dinghy and should be held by an adult on the boat as the child either enters or leaves it. Likewise, an adult ashore should take charge when the dinghy is alongside a pontoon or quay. This leaves the adult in the dinghy with one hand to help the child and another to keep the dinghy steady.

The last stage of being Very Young is the most active and now we must be ashore rather more than before. Children of three and four love to play on the beach and in the mud. This is probably the best time to start teaching them how to swim. Almost certainly passages will have to be either made at night or kept very short indeed. However, the child is now old enough to start learning to use its own safety belt, clipping itself from one point to another as it moves around the deck. It may be that the usual harness clips are too tough for little fingers and will have to be replaced with ones that they can manage. Since the harness will not be expected to cope with the very severe conditions for which they must be designed, 'down grading' a clip will not put the child at risk and it is far more important that they learn the safety-belt habit.

Youngsters of this age are delightfully curious and will want to know exactly what you are doing. Instruction should be by showing them slowly and carefully, not by constantly telling them 'don't' this and 'don't' that. You are laying the foundations and as children of this age are very impressionable the impression you want to make is that sailing is fun and not an almighty bore.

And Now We Are Six (with apologies to A. A. Milne)

At quite an early age, a child needs a bit of the boat which is private. This will be centred around his (or her, but we'll use just 'his' as it's shorter) bunk and should include at least a locker where special treasures such as shells and dead snakes can be kept. If a curtain can be rigged up so that the bunk is a truly private place, so much the better. Like all of us, the child is a territorial animal and it is a small price to pay to keep the youngster happy.

Since the bunk is the place where young children tend to go when weather conditions are bad, and as we all know that a tired child is a pretty objectionable beast, the bunk must be both comfortable and secure. Lee boards tend to be a bit hard and a canvas lee cloth rigged up using small jambing cleats so that the occupant can tighten it up is ideal. If fitted properly, the cloth can be dropped down out of the way during the day so that the bunk becomes a seat.

Many small children demand a great deal of attention and most parents are only too familiar with those two battle cries: 'I'm bored!' and 'What shall we do now?' For some reason many parents who are happy to entertain their children when ashore seem to think that the same child afloat will require less company. Bearing in mind that television is a large part of the leisure hours of many children, the reverse is far more likely to be true.

There is not room on board to carry a wealth of board games. Cards take little space and can provide hours of fun – we always carry at least three packs in case of accidents and the odd lost King – whilst a small chess set is also invaluable if this game appeals. The only large board game we take with us is Scrabble but that is, of course, a very personal choice. Books, on the other hand, are vital. These should fall into two categories – reference works and yarns. The former should include books which identify all the various things which are likely to be encountered. The Observer books are ideal for a start as the range covers *Birds* (1), *Wild Flowers* (2), *Butterflies* (3), *Trees* (4),

Ships (15), *Weather* (22), *Sea Fishes* (28), *Flags* (29) and *Sea & Seashore* (31), the numbers in brackets being the Observer reference numbers. Using these books, children should be encouraged to keep a log of all they find and discover. If they can be persuaded to illustrate this with sketches and drawings, so much the better.

Fishing can be a great diversion even when utterly pointless. Our son will spend hours fishing for crabs using a piece of bacon rind tied to a piece of string – always assuming that the crabs are feeling co-operative! However, the greatest diversion from the children's point of view is the dinghy.

As soon as the children are old enough and skilled enough to handle the dinghy on their own – and this can be achieved surprisingly quickly – the boat should be turned over to them and become their responsibility. In many dinghies, a better balance is achieved if the youngster (or even youngsters) are on the centre thwart rowing with an adult in both bows and stern. Almost nothing can give the same sense of pride to a child than to be able to row his parents ashore. By trading on this sense of pride, the children will soon consider the appearance of the dinghy and enjoy keeping it spick and span. It is possible to extend this thought and let them carry out the winter maintenance, scraping down and repainting or revarnishing. The dinghy should be able to sail. All that is required is a simple lugsail although older children will soon demand something with a jib so that they can take part in any local regatta you may come across in your travels. That, however, is a problem that can be deferred until they are in their early teens.

Children in harbour can be charming or unholy terrors. In many ports it will be necessary to tie up alongside another vessel whose crew may be sleeping after a long and tiring passage and will not appreciate children bouncing and thudding over their deck. By the same token, transistor radios blaring, noisy deck games and rowdy squabbles should be banned. If the children are suffering from a surfeit of energy, they should go ashore to work it off. Again, the dinghy can provide the main focal point for their activity as most ports and harbours offer them the prospect of exploring. Whether or not one allows one's children to visit other boats is a matter for personal choice, but it should be avoided unless you are prepared to act as host to their friends as well. Children can be very sensitive if they feel they cannot reciprocate hospitality.

Although I am strongly against régimes which impose very strict discipline on children, and parents who are for ever telling their children not to do this and not to do that, there are a few basic rules which must be followed for the sake of safety. Children should not be allowed on deck without an adult when under way and should wear harnesses at all times when outside the cabin – and that includes when they are in the cockpit. A lifejacket should be worn at all times when in the dinghy. Lastly, children should always stow all books and toys when they have finished playing with them. This may not seem to be associated with safety and for much of the time it isn't. However, I remember getting very wet one fine night as I went forward in the gloaming to light – belatedly – the anchor light. As I walked confidently along the side deck, my foot suddenly shot out from underneath me and I slipped over the side. It was a combination of my own carelessness and standing on a small toy car which skidded out from below my unsuspecting foot.

Whilst on the subject of stowage and children, there is also a very definite rule that should apply to adults. Many accidents occur because tools are left where they should not be left. A small, bare foot standing on the corner of a sharp triangular scraper can be badly cut. It is very good practice to make a thorough check whenever any work has been carried out to ensure that all tools etc are cleared away afterwards.

Crew Strength and Watchkeeping

Most folk who take up cruising vastly overestimate the strength of their crew. This results in over-ambitious plans and tired, which means danger-prone, crewmembers.

Whilst it is true that a fully fit and very experienced person can sail almost non-stop, very few people who are cruising are either fully fit or very experienced. Although it is possible to stand a watch of as long as 24 hours in fine weather and get away with it, the longest watch which can be considered safe, even in fine weather, is 12 hours. Even this presupposes that one is not tired at the start and will be able to sleep it off afterwards. So much for theory, now the reality.

It is not our job as skipper of a cruising boat to prove how good we are but to ensure the safe conduct of our ship at all times. Until other members of the crew have sufficient experience to stand watches, the weight will fall almost entirely on the skipper. This is not to say that others will not be taking a trick at the helm and helping on deck, it is to say that the skipper will have to remain alert all the time the ship is under way. Under these circumstances, I would limit the time under way to 70 hours in a fortnight's cruise – an average of 5 hours per day. At an average speed of 3 knots that would mean just over 200 miles. This is ample for a first cruise, especially as there will be dinghy sailing and training as well. Obviously one would not be sailing for 5 hours every day and some longer passages could be considered. A 12-hour passage is perfectly safe so long as the days either side are not too active.

As the mate becomes more experienced, this figure can be increased to 90 hours, but even when the crew includes a couple of well-trained teenagers as well, 140 hours per fortnight is a sensible limit. Any attempt to exceed this figure – roughly 40 per cent of the total time – will turn the cruise into hard work although I must admit that some folk thoroughly enjoy the challenge of cruising rather than the peaceful approach and would sneer at such a suggestion.

Watchkeeping should be introduced for any passage of more than 4 hours. It may well be, of course, that the skipper will be on duty for the entire passage in the early days but the rest of the crew should still operate on a rota basis.

If the crew consists of our standard family, divide the total time of the proposed passage by 4. The resulting figure cannot exceed 3 hours if we are sensibly keeping the total passage to under 12 hours. Each child should stand watch for a quarter of the time and the mate for a half. However, small children will become bored and tired after about 1½ hours and so the watch bill could be something like this:

0–1½   Skipper plus one child
1½–3   Skipper plus second child
3–6   Skipper plus mate
6–7½   Skipper plus first child
7½–9   Skipper plus second child
9–12   Skipper plus mate

Such an arrangement would give the skipper a chance to take a break during the period 3–6 hours and would mean that both adults are on watch towards the end of the passage when the skipper is feeling tired.

As the mate and the children become more experienced so they can take more of the load and I have one friend who operates rather like a naval captain. He keeps no watches at all as such and splits passages into 3-hour periods. The mate and children take each watch in turn (the children being about fifteen and thirteen when he began this system) and call him whenever one of a number of circumstances warrants his attention. He keeps a list pinned up which, if my memory serves me, reads like this:

Any change in wind direction or force
Any sighting of another vessel or a navigational aid
Whenever a course change is required
Any sign of gear failing or coming adrift
Whenever the watchkeeper is feeling too tired to continue

Our children are too young to consider such a system but it is worth thinking about as it does mean the skipper is there, and in good fettle, whenever his presence is required. It also breeds a sense of responsibility in the crew and gives them a feeling of pride.

Incidentally, although he runs a very tight ship, none of the crew seems to object. Indeed, I am sure they enjoy being part of the only crew that I know that can come alongside under sail and make fast etc without a word being spoken. Father, sitting at the helm – and wearing a Panama hat if the weather is decent – just nods and lifts the occasional finger and everything happens as if by magic.

The exact watch bill will depend greatly on the crew and must be tailored to suit them. I believe that flexibility is very important as 'crew strength' can vary almost daily. The important points to watch for are accumulated tiredness and the need to provide the children with time ashore.

Appendices

I CLOTHING

Much has been written about clothing suitable for cruising. Personally, I see no reason why folk shouldn't wear exactly what they want to. If you wish to belong to a sailing club and wear the latest sailing fashions there are a host of shops waiting to fill your matching waterproof holdalls. If, like me, you cruise to leave people behind, your attitude will be very different and you will wear just what you want to.

The three rules are: keep warm, be comfortable, keep dry. The first can be achieved by wearing special underwear such as the Lifa range by Helly-Hansen which has the advantage that it helps to keep you dry thanks to its tendency to pass moisture one way only – outwards (it works rather like a baby's nappy liner). Using such underwear will reduce the number of other garments required, another plus. We find that we prefer to stick to natural fibres and layers of fairly lightweight cotton and wool seem to work best. A cotton T-shirt followed by a light wool jersey, a cotton shirt, a medium-weight sweater and a boiler suit over everything is my own recipe. The lower end is covered with thick cavalry twill trousers when it's very cold and rather lighter flannels at other times. It is all a matter of taste.

Comfort can be destroyed by trying to wear clothing which is too tight. I am amazed whenever I see people sailing in tight jeans – and that goes for the girls as well as the men. The looser cotton sailing trousers overcome this problem but my wife seems to favour track suits and she, too, often tops the lot with an ordinary boiler suit. Incidentally, she finds full-length wool skirts the warmest and most comfortable thing to wear when in port.

You will gather that boiler suits loom large in our life. This is because they are fairly windproof, can be worn with either everything or nothing underneath (my wife has a pair of 'fashion' boiler suits which are smaller and worn in summer) and have plenty of pockets – a great advantage.

Children can become frozen when they turn in and so it often pays to let them dress with their pyjamas underneath so that they do not have to undress.

Footwear is one area where one should look at special designs. The soles should be non-slip and offer a good grip. Proper sailing shoes may be bought with both canvas and leather uppers, the latter being in the form of bootees. Although leather sailing shoes are expensive they are much warmer than either canvas shoes or boots. Boots should not have insteps as these can catch and be dangerous – again there is merit at looking at those designed for the job.

Keeping dry is the hardest part. Totally waterproof garments tend to make one perspire freely and the ventilation holes cannot be made large enough to cope. Another problem is that one-piece suits or chest-high trousers make going to the loo a complicated process. I have found chest-high trousers with an anorak the best solution as waist trousers are both uncomfortable and offer a gap into which every passing slop will find a way. Since zips are difficult for wet and cold fingers to work and often jamb, I always look for drawstrings. This is even more important where children are concerned as they find most zips impossible.

For going ashore in the dinghy and just plodding around generally, we find long macintoshes worn with knee-length boots better than the more usual gear. Apart from reducing the problems of perspiration, a standard macintosh gives you somewhere to tuck the shopping away in the dry. They are, however, fairly useless when the wind is blowing very hard.

In this country we tend to think much more about the wet and the cold than we do about the sun. However, we do see the odd good summer and then the problems are rather different. The combination of sun and sea wind can play havoc with sensitive untrained skin and induce heavy, throbbing headaches. A hat with a good wide brim can make life a lot easier. Best is an old-fashioned white sun hat as this will reflect the heat and keep the wearer's head much cooler. In these conditions loose, light-coloured clothing will be needed until a tan enables one to wear a pair of trunks or a bikini. Remember, however, that a tight pair of trunks or a tight bikini bottom can make one very sore if it contains salt – and few clothes worn at sea are absolutely free from it.

In addition to clothes for normal wear, there should be at least one set of 'oldies' per person for the odd very mucky job like scrubbing the bottom or seeing to a recalcitrant engine. At the other end of the scale, one set of respectable shore-going togs is advisable – you never know, you may want to go to a dance or out for dinner. Stowing such clothes can be a problem unless they can be kept on hangers in a suitable waterproof bag. One of the folding suitcases that have hangers inside and can be strung up by a ring can be used to hold everyone's Number Ones if there is a large enough hanging locker to accommodate it. Sadly, few of these are fitted with a hanging ring strong enough to withstand the rigours of life at sea and it may require reinforcing or even replacing.

II FIRST-AID AND SEASICKNESS

Unlike the trans-oceanic cruising fraternity, those wandering around the coasts are rarely far from medical aid. However, accidents do happen and it is essential that at least one person (far better if it is two, it may be the first-aid pundit is the one knocked unconscious) has a good working knowledge of first-aid procedures. The St John Ambulance run first-aid courses in most towns from time to time and offer excellent training. It costs only a few pounds and a few evenings, and can mean you are able to save a life – perhaps a life very close and dear to you. At the end of the course there is an examination and those who pass are issued with a certificate which is valid for three years after which a refresher course must be attended. I hate linking the thought of any legislation with cruising as it remains one of the few areas of life which is unencumbered by the law; if, however, legislation were to be introduced, I would advocate that all skippers of cruising boats carry a valid St John Ambulance certificate.

If the above course is followed, you will end up with a copy of the St John *First Aid Manual*. If, however, you do not a similar work should be bought. The almanacs contain a section on first-aid which covers most requirements but is not really an adequate alternative. It is, of course, pointless to buy a manual and wait until it is needed before opening it. At least it should be read through a couple of times so that one is familiar with the contents and knows where to find whatever is required.

A good first-aid kit should be carried. It is possible to buy ready-made kits neatly packed in tins but these do not leave room for the extras that one wants to carry and I find it better to use an old (and large) ice-cream container which keeps everything dry. A list of contents follows, but don't forget the odds and ends needed by your particular crew. Any medicines etc that need to be kept available at home should be included – and properly marked.

First-aid Kit for a Crew of Four including Children

2   triangular bandages
1   55mm crêpe bandage
1   100mm crêpe bandage
1   50mm gauze bandage
1   75mm roll Elastoplast
5   packs steristrips
10 100 × 100mm gauze dressings
10 50 × 50mm gauze dressings
5   packs sterile paraffin-gauze burn dressings
—   assorted Elastoplast dressings (the more the merrier)
—   cotton wool
2   good stainless steel scissors (small and large)
1   pair stainless steel tweezers
—   safety pins
2   tubes disinfectant cleansing agent (eg Savlon)
—   antibiotic powder (eg Alficetyn – prescription required)
2   tins soothing cream (eg Germolene)
2   tubes Anthisan (for bites and stings)
1   plastic tub Paracetamol (pain killer)
—   Pentazocine (strong pain killer – prescription required)
—   calamine lotion (for sunburn)
1   tin petroleum jelly (also ideal for on-board lubrication jobs)

The above list, together with seasickness tablets and any special medicines that may be required, should suffice for short coastal cruises. It is rather heavy on bandages as these tend to be the ones that are not replaced when used and a fair number are required if someone breaks a bone and slings and splints have to be used. For longer cruises, consult the almanac for extended list or purchase one of the kits designed to Department of Trade requirements for fishing boats.

A special kit for yachts is marketed by Simpson-Lawrence Ltd under the name Practica.

Seasickness

Ninety-five per cent of the population suffer to a greater or lesser extent from seasickness and so it is nothing to be ashamed of. Luckily only about 10 per cent suffer badly and never seem to be free from it even after a long period afloat. There are a number of causes: motion, noise, smells, fumes, over-eating, alcohol (especially in excess), cold, wetness, hunger and tiredness are the most common of these.

Some causes are clearly avoidable. For twelve hours or so before setting off diets should be kept very plain and simple – starvation being quite acceptable. Seasickness pills can be taken about four hours before leaving and the fact that they have been taken seems to help some people almost as much as the pills themselves. There are a number of different seasickness tablets available and only trial and error will show which suits each individual. It is fatal to wait until sickness starts and then to take a tablet; it only makes matters worse and the odds are that one will be sick again before the tablet has been digested.

If any member of the crew continues to suffer it is well worth trying to find out the cause and then doing something about it along the following lines:

Motion   Try a different part of the boat. A move from one side to the other for a couple of days may cure the patient even if it does disrupt the sleeping arrangements.
Noise   Try ear plugs. These can be made from cotton wool.
Smells   Usually associated with the engine oil or fuel and caused by leaks or spillage. In any event, these should be cured and avoided.
Fumes   Exhaust fumes are the usual culprit. Check for leaks but it may be that they are being blown back on board. Modifying the outlet may help but in the final analysis this problem may be difficult to overcome when using the engine under certain conditions. Try sailing – it saves on fuel and is far quieter anyway.
Over-eating   They say that every vice brings its own reward.
Alcohol   As for over-eating but even more so.
Cold   In extreme cases bundle the sufferer into a sleeping bag without undressing him and add a couple of hot-water bottles which should be carried for just this reason.
Wetness   Strip the sufferer and rub down with a towel; then treat as for cold.
Hunger   This is the hardest cause to overcome as some people just do not want to eat for a couple of days when the sickness is caused by the unfamiliar surroundings and then find they remain sick through hunger and yet still cannot face food. Little and often is the best solution and dry

biscuits often prove most acceptable. Some folk find that barley sugar and glucose tablets help.

Tiredness Obviously no cure, it just has to be avoided.

If one is feeling slightly sick, the best solution is to keep busy. Many sufferers have been saved by an observant skipper finding a suitable job at the critical moment. Often the best job is to take the helm – the skipper can always find some other job that suddenly needs his attention such as checking some point on the chart. Most people find it easier to stay on deck but if they are getting too cold or wet they should be sent below where lying down may make them feel better. In any event, most will wish to retire to their bunk if the attack is a bad one.

We all know the result of being sick to windward but it is always safer to be sick into a handily placed bucket than over the rail. I once spent an evening with a US Coastguard who told me that the main cause of drowning in his area was men relieving themselves over the side and this was closely followed by folk being sick over the side. He may or may not have been telling the truth, but it is worth thinking about.

III EMERGENCY-GEAR CHECKLIST

Trysail and gear ('gear' will include special sheets etc required).
Storm jib and gear.
Storm anchor (shackled to chain and lashed on foredeck. Chain should have been properly stowed but, if not, should be overhauled and re-stowed).
Drogue (or sea anchor) and warps, including tripping line.
Spare warps (for streaming when running).
Jackstays rigged and safety harnesses available.
All deck fastenings and lashings in order.
All rope tails secured.
Bunk lee boards or canvasses rigged.
All items below decks properly secured.
Thermos flasks filled with hot drinks (and stew if required).
Engine started and tested.

Damage Control

Tools
Bolt cutters (for cutting adrift rigging).
Pliers.
Heavy screwdriver.
Spanners (or adjustable spanner).
Hammer and saw.
Fire extinguishers.

Materials
Hanks of various sizes of rope down to twine.

'Fothers': pieces of canvas of double thickness with heavy-duty polyethylene sheet stitched between them and fitted with eyelets on each corner; of various sizes to put over hull damage.

Timbers: a few lengths of 2" × 2" are best. These, together with the next item, can be used to brace under damaged coachroofs, across the boat if a frame breaks and the hull starts to collapse or even to support a piece of plywood used inside a hole.

Wedges: invaluable and not easy to make in a hurry.

Plywood: ¼" thick is best as it is flexible enough to take quite sharp curves. A few pieces about 2ft square will do.

Bag with some spare blocks and shackles.

Tin with a selection of screws, copper nails and nuts, washers and bolts.

Personal Damage Control

First-aid kit and medical kit. This will depend on the crew's personal requirements and is covered in Appendix II.

Attracting Attention

Radio: on Channel 16.

Flares: at least 12 assorted.

Daylight orange smoke signals.

Powerful torch (batteries checked).

International Code Flags 'V' (I require assistance) and 'N' over 'C' (I am in distress and require immediate assistance).

Abandoning Ship

The harnesses which have been keeping you firmly attached are no longer of assistance. Lifejackets must be worn.

Liferaft (or inflatable) with the following:

Fresh water (the first 'must': one can last a long time without food and for a very short time without water). Best in containers attached to raft.

Warm clothing and some blankets. The second 'must' is to keep warm – in the tropics, cool – and clothing/blankets must be both wind and waterproof (it is assumed that the crew will be wearing 'oilies'). Best kept in heavy-duty polyethylene bags inside canvas bags, attached to liferaft by short lines.

Flares, smoke signals. Kept in water-tight screw-lid container attached to liferaft.

Torch(es) and spare batteries. May be stowed with flares.

Food. Thermos flasks with hot drinks and stews are excellent but there is rarely time to prepare them and they are vulnerable to damage. Dried foods (biscuits, fruits – including raisins, dates etc – chocolate and 'heavy' cake such as fruit cake) in screw-top containers.

First-aid and medical kit.

(This list is not comprehensive and items such as fishing lines should be added if cruising far from land. The radio is not included but should be carried if it runs off its own power and carries its own aerial – special radio distress beacons are available to assist Search and Rescue services to locate the liferaft.)

Naturally it will not be possible to stow all the above in either the liferaft or the inflatable as a matter of course. The various containers should be available, with the lines required to attach them, at all times ready to receive their contents. These lines can be attached to a single warp which is made fast to the liferaft or inflatable as it is launched and the items collected aboard as required.

It is strongly advised that inflatables are fitted with a drogue to reduce drift (liferafts should have one as part of the standard equipment) and paddles should be taken if possible. The chances are that progress will be almost impossible – especially in a liferaft – and that the energy used would be better employed in keeping warm. However, the ability to make some progress may make the difference between a safe and a disastrous landing and, in a few cases, between being rescued and passed by unseen.

IV RESCUE SERVICES

HM Coastguard

HM Coastguard is responsible for all Search and Rescue operations at sea. To assist in its task it calls on the services of the RNLI, local fishing craft, RN and RAF helicopters and so on, as well as using its own men and equipment. However, no rescue can be attempted until a missing craft is located.

To help in searching for missing craft, HM Coastguard runs schemes whereby it carries details of vessels on its files. The exact details of these schemes are varied from time to time and full information should be obtained from the nearest Coastguard Station. There was a time when one reported departures and arrivals direct to the coastguards who would initiate a search if one was overdue. However, partly owing to the vast increase in small boats cruising around the coasts and partly owing to the sad fact that some people abused the system, this no longer applies. Now it is up to the skipper to nominate a contact ashore who will contact the coastguard on his behalf if he fails to arrive when expected. A search will then commence as soon as possible.

This places two duties on the skipper. On arrival he must get in touch with his shore contact to avoid a needless search. The importance of this cannot be overstated. The second duty is to limit the area of search as much as possible. This can be achieved in two ways. A 'passage plan' can be lodged with the shore contact – ensuring that it is brought up to date whenever the plan is varied – and HM Coastguard can be informed of the boat's position from time to time. This is, of course, far easier if a radio is carried (use Channel 67) but if not a quick telephone call to the nearest coastguard station just prior to departure must suffice. Such calls will be noted in the coastguard's logbook and will be available if required.

Coastguards are always willing to offer free advice and guidance to all cruising folk – but it is up to the skipper to make the first contact with them.

The Royal National Lifeboat Institution

The RNLI is probably one of the most incredible organisations that has ever existed. Run purely on voluntary subscriptions with no formal aid from any statutory body or government department, the men and equipment stand by twenty-four hours a day, seven days a week, ready and willing to put to sea to save any life regardless of race, colour or creed at no cost to those saved.

If such a service were to be run by an insurance company, the premiums required would be astronomical and doubtless beyond the means of most cruising skippers. The cost of running the Institution is staggering: a new Arun Lifeboat, for example, carries a price tag of £350,000. Once launched on a rescue mission, a boat will stand by, just in case. It could be that its first call will be to come and rescue you – and your wife and children.

The organisation set up to support the RNLI is called 'Shoreline'. Membership is from £5.00 per annum for a single person, from £7.50 for Family Membership. It is a small price to pay for the security that comes from knowing that the lifeboats and crews are there. Full details can be obtained from The Director, RNLI, West Quay Road, Poole, Dorset, BH15 1HZ.

Bibliography and Useful Addresses

Of General Interest

Hiscock, Eric C., *Cruising Under Sail* (Oxford University Press, 1965)
Hiscock needs no introduction and few who enjoy cruising will be without this book. It is very comprehensive but can be enjoyed fully only by those with some experience.

Hollander, Neil, and Mertes, Harald, *The Yachtsman's Emergency Handbook* (Angus & Robertson, 1980)
This is an extraordinary book. It looks at a host of disasters, some small, some catastrophic, and offers solutions, solutions based on the experience of a wide variety of seamen. It should not remain on the bookshelves when one is at sea but should stand alongside the almanac over the chart table.

Russell, John, *The Shell Book of Seamanship* (David & Charles, 1979)
A delightful book to browse through, it offers something for all from the novice to the most experienced.

Tabarly, Eric, *Practical Yacht Handling* (Stanford Maritime)
Packed full of good advice from one of the great small-boat seamen, this offers the reader a wide range of subjects from manoeuvring to jury rigs.

Ropes and Ropework

Ropes have been described as the sinews of the sailing craft. Certainly it is true that without a comprehensive knowledge of their qualities and the various ways in which they can be used, the seaman's education is sorely lacking. Either of the following will prove of value and will enhance the seaman's enjoyment by teaching him to make the most of his 'sinews'.

Fry, Eric C. and Wilson, Peter J., *The Shell Combined Book of Knots and Ropework (Practical and Decorative)* (David & Charles, 1981)

Maclean, William P., *Modern Marlinspike Seamanship* (David & Charles, 1982)

Weather Forecasting

Glénans Weather Forecasting: A Manual for Yachtsmen (David & Charles, 1980)

Written by a team from the famous French sailing centre at Glénans, this book deals with the subject very fully and although it requires some close attention it does offer a thorough understanding of this complex and fascinating subject.

Sanderson, Ray, *Meteorology for Yachtsmen* (Stanford Maritime)
Ray Sanderson is a professional forecaster and a yachtsman. He tackles the subject in language that the layman can understand with little difficulty.

Navigation

Navigation is not the mystery that it is often considered to be but it must be admitted that suggesting books on the subject is fraught with difficulty as some readers find one approach easy to understand while others prefer a very different style. However, one of the following should suit all tastes.

Blewitt, Mary, *Navigation for Yachtsmen* (Stanford Maritime, 1972)
An untheoretical approach to the problem which emphasises the practical problems.

Fraser, Bruce, *Weekend Navigator* (Adlard Coles, 1981)
Written with the novice in mind, it endeavours to avoid making the subject more complex than is necessary.

Navigation: An RYA Manual (David & Charles, 1981)
This book is based on the syllabus for the RYA/DoT Yachtmaster Offshore Certificate.

Toghill, Jeff, *The Yachtsman's Navigation Manual* (Ward Lock, 1980)
Well illustrated, this covers equipment, weather forecasting and celestial navigation as well as offering more basic information.

Almanacs

The Macmillan & Silk Cut Nautical Almanac (Macmillan)
Reed's Nautical Almanac (Thomas Reed Publications)

Pilots

There are a number of pilots printed which offer details of sections of our coastline. However, the only pilot which covers the entire UK is the Cruising Association Handbook published by the Cruising Association in London.

Medical

Counter, Dr R. T., *The Yachtsman's Doctor* (Nautical Publishing Co)

First Aid (the authorised manual of St John Ambulance Association and Brigade)

Equipment

Bowyer, Peter, *Boat Engines* (David & Charles, 1979)
   This takes a degree of concentration if it is to be understood but it covers the subject very fully and is well worth the effort.

French, John, *Electrics and Electronics for Small Craft* (Adlard Coles, 1981)
   A comprehensive consideration of the subject which may, on occasion, prove rather hard work.

Jarman, Colin (ed), *Sailing and Boating: The Complete Equipment Guide* (David & Charles, 1981)

The above selection of books hardly scratches the surface for there is a wealth of information which has been published. However, no list can hope to be complete and I trust that the authors and publishers of the many excellent books I have not mentioned will forgive me. I have offered those which have proved of most value to me.

Useful Addresses

Balance Engineering, 135 Cambridge Road, New Wimpole, Cambridgeshire. Tel (022020) 482 (*see Plate 11.2*)
Blake & Sons (Gosport) Ltd, Park Road, Gosport, Hampshire. Tel (07017) 23411 (*see Plate 11.4*)
Bruce Anchor Ltd, Northfield Broadway, Edinburgh, EH8 7RY. Tel (031) 669 6121 (*see Plate 2.8*)
Cruising Association, Ivory House, St Katharine's Dock, London E1 9AT. Tel (01) 481 0881
Honda UK Ltd, Power Road, Chiswick, London W4. Tel (01) 995 9381 (*see Plate 11.1*)
Imray, Laurie, Norie & Wilson Ltd, Wych House, St Ives, Huntingdon, Cambridgeshire. Tel (0480) 62114
Isaiah Preston Ltd, Station Street, Cradley Heath, W. Midlands. Tel (0384) 65415 (*see Plate 2.6*)
Joy & King Ltd, 15 Alperton Lane, Perivale, Greenford, Middlesex. Tel (01) 997 5653 (*see Plate 11.5*)
Lo-Kata Ltd, Falmouth, Cornwall, TR10 8AR. Tel (0326) 73636 (*see Plate 10.1*)
Simpson Lawrence Ltd, 218/228 Edmiston Drive, Glasgow, G51 2YT. Tel (041) 427 5331 (*see Plates 2.1, 2.2, 2.3, 2.4, 2.7, 5.1, 5.2, 5.3, 5.4, 5.5, 5.6, 5.7 and 5.13*)
South Western Marine Factors, Pottery Road, Poole, Dorset. Tel (0202) 745414 (*see Plates 3.1, 5.8, 5.9, 5.10, 5.12, 8.1 and 11.3*)
Stanford Maritime, 12/14 Long Acre, London WC2E 9LP. Tel (01) 836 7863
Thomas Walker & Son Ltd, 58 Oxford Street, Birmingham, B5 5NX. Tel (021) 643 5474 (*see Plate 5.11*)

Index

Aids to navigation, 100ff
Alcohol cooking stoves, 159
Almanac, nautical, 52, 79, 80
Anchor, backing up the, 20ff
  bower, 9, 13, 33
  Bruce, 12ff
  buoy, 17
  cable, 9ff, 14ff, 34ff
  cable, scope of, 14
  cable, stowage, 15, 34ff
  Danforth, 12ff, 33
  fisherman, 10ff
  handling, 26, 30ff
  holding power, 14
  kedge, 9, 13, 33
  light, 23, 136
  plough, 11ff, 33
  shape, 23, 136
  sizes, 25
  stockless, 12ff
  storm, 10ff, 33
  stowage, 32ff
  tripping line, 17, 30ff
  weighing, 26, 30ff
  winch, 27ff
Anchoring, 16ff
Avoiding collision, 126ff

Bad weather, 116ff
Bearings, cross, 56, 72ff
Berthing, 43ff
Bower anchor, 9, 13, 33
Bow roller, 26
Bruce anchor, 12ff
Bunk, leeboards, 122ff
Buoy, anchor, 17
  mooring, 37ff
  navigation, 105ff

Cable, anchor, 9ff, 14ff, 34ff
  scope of, 14
  stowage of, 15, 34ff
Charts, 52, 77ff
Chartwork, 52ff
  notations, 60ff
  plotting ship's track, 58ff
Circular notation, 56, 82
Clothing, 180ff
Code, International, 141ff
Communications, 133ff
Compass correction, 82
  deviation, 68
  error, 67ff, 73, 82
  error table, 70ff
  hand bearing, 72, 87, 89

  lighting, 87
  notation, circular, 56, 82
    quadrantal, 82
  steering, 81ff
  swinging, 68ff
Cooking, 160ff
Cooking stoves, 158ff
Course, 55ff
Course to steer, plotting, 62ff
Course Table, 63ff
Crew, 165ff
  fear in, 122
  hunger in, 124ff
  physical state of, 121ff
  strength of, 177ff
  tiredness in, 122ff
  training of, 166ff

Danforth anchor, 12ff, 33
Day Marks, 105ff, 136ff
Dead Reckoning, 59
Deck log, 66
Distance off, 74ff
Distress signals, 140ff

Echo sounder, 16, 75, 90ff
Electricity, 147ff
Emergency gear, 119, 121, 184ff
Estimated Position, 60, 73

Fear, 122
Fenders, 45ff
First Aid, 181ff
Fisherman anchor, 10ff

Gas cookers, 159
Gas heaters, 156
Give-way order, 131
Give-way zones, 131
Gnomonic Projection, 78
Grab handles, 123

Hand-bearing compass, 72, 87, 89
Heating, 155ff
HM Coastguard, 186
Holding power of anchors, 14
Hot-air heaters, 157
Hunger, 124ff

International Code, 141ff
International Regulations for Preventing
  Collisions at Sea, 126ff

Kedge, 9, 13, 33
Knot, measurement of speed, 55ff

Lead and line, 16ff, 93ff
Leading marks, 106ff
Leeway, 66
Life raft, 121, 185
Lights, anchor, 23, 136
   buoy and coastal, 100ff
   cabin, 153ff
   compass, 87
   navigation, 134ff
Log, 56, 72, 95ff
Log books, 99
Log books, deck, 66

Magnetic Variation, 68
Manoeuvring, 36, 38, 48ff
Mercator's Projection, 77
Mooring buoys, 37ff
Moorings, picking up, 37ff

Nautical Almanacs, 52, 79, 80
Nautical miles, 55
Navigation, 52ff
Navigation buoys, 105ff
Notices to Mariners, 81

Paraffin cookers, 158
Paraffin heaters, 156
Parallel rules, 58
Passage planning, 60ff
Pelorus, 68, 72, 87ff
Perches, 107ff
Pilotage, 52ff
Pilots, 81
Plotting course to steer, 62ff
Plotting ship's track, 58ff
Plough anchor, 11ff, 33
Poor visibility, 125, 128, 140
Position lines, 56, 72, 74ff

Quadrantal Notation, 82ff

Radio, 143ff
Radio Direction Finding, 145
Right of Way, 127, 131ff
Royal National Lifeboat Institution, 187

Running fix, 74ff

Safety harness, 119ff
Sailing Directions, 81
Scope, of anchor cable, 14
Sea sickness, 183ff
Shapes, 136
Shapes, anchor, 23, 136
Ship's position, fixing of, 55ff, 65, 72ff
Ship's track, plotting of, 58ff
Signals, distress, 140ff
Signals, sound, 137, 140
Slow-speed working, 36, 38, 48ff
Solid-fuel cookers, 159
Solid-fuel heating, 155
Sound signals, 137, 140
Speed indicators (logs), 56, 72, 95ff
Steering compass, 81ff
Stem fittings, 26
Stockless anchor, 12ff
Storm anchor, 10, 13, 33
Stowage, anchors, 32ff
   anchor cables, 15, 34ff
   in bad weather, 118ff

Tidal atlases, 81
Tidal flow, 57
Tidal flow, effect of, 58ff
Tides, 57ff, 81, 109ff
Tides, calculating height of, 113ff
   terms and definitions, 112ff
Tiredness, 122, 124
Toilets, 163ff
Traffic Separation Schemes, 130ff
Traffic Signals, 108
Transferred Position Lines, 74ff
Transits, 69, 72

Warping, 48
Warps, 43ff
Watchkeeping, 60ff, 177
Water storage and systems, 161ff
Weather, bad, 116ff
   forecasts, 117ff
Winch, anchor, 27ff